Robin

340 Hunico Lr.

McDonough, GA

30252

April 21st 2022

William Spurstone died of
the bubonic plague that
lasted a year 1665 - 1666
in London.
" Black Death "

MW00780696

The Wiles of
Satan

A discourse on 2 Corinthians 2:11: "Lest Satan
should get an advantage of us, for we are
not ignorant of his devices."

by

William Spurstowe, D. D.
Minister at Hackney

"Be sober, be vigilant; because your adversary the devil,
as a roaring lion, walketh about seeking whom he
may devour: whom resist stedfast in the faith. . . ."
1 Peter 5:8–9

Edited by Dr. Don Kistler

Soli Deo Gloria Publication
. . . for instruction in righteousness . . .

Soli Deo Gloria Publications
A division of Soli Deo Gloria Ministries, Inc.
P. O. Box 451, Morgan PA 15064
(412) 221-1901/FAX 221-1902
www.SDGbooks.com

*

*

ISBN 1-57358-163-1

*

Library of Congress Cataloging-in-Publication Data

Spurstowe, William, 1644 or 5-1654.
 The Wiles of Satan : a discourse on 2 Corinthians 2:11 / by
William Spurstowe ; edited by Don Kistler.– 1st American ed.
   p. cm.
 ISBN 1-57358-163-1 (alk. paper)
 1. Bible. N.T. Corinthians, 2nd, II, 11–Criticism, interpretation,
etc.
 2. Devil–Biblical teaching. 3. Spiritual warfare. I. Kistler, Don.
II.
 Title.
BS2675.52.S68 2004
235'.4–dc22

                                         2004008555

Contents

The Life and Writings of William Spurstowe

William Spurstowe was born around 1605, the eldest son and heir of William Spurstowe, Sr., a London merchant, and the grandson of Thomas Spurstowe, of Shrewsbury. His mother, Damoris Parkhurst of Gilford had many ties to Puritan families in both old and New England. Spurstowe had three brothers (Henry, Samuel, Joseph) and one sister, Olive. His father was a member of John Davenport's congregation and witnessed Davenport sign the Four Articles, which proposed the governance of Connecticut; later Spurstowe, Sr., served as the member for Shrewsbury in the Long Parliament.

Spurstowe was sent to Emmanuel College, Cambridge, in 1623, and earned his B.A. in 1627. He was incorporated at Oxford in 1628. He moved to St. Catherine's College, and there received his M.A. in 1630. He became a Fellow of St. Catherine's in 1638 and a Master of the college in 1645. He was approved Master of Clare on April 22, 1645, but the appointment was given to Ralph Cudworth. From St. Catherine's, a budding Puritan institution then under the Mastership of Richard Sibbes, Spurstowe accepted the call to the rectory of Great Hampden, Buckinghamshire, where John Hampden, the great Parliamentary leader was a member. Spurstowe was officially installed on June 30, 1638, but most likely began preaching there a year earlier. Sometime around 1640, Spurstowe married a young woman named Sarah (her surname is not known), a godly, virtuous, and kind woman. She was then twenty years old.

Spurstowe's rise to public preferment was probably at the hand of Hampden, who was so well known and admired that he was able to get William Laud and Thomas Wentworth arrested and sent to the Tower of London. During the early Civil Wars (1642–1643), Spurstowe was chaplain to Hampden's regiment of "green coats." Spurstowe, like Hampden, hoped to overthrow the king's forces in order to push the sovereign to a position more favorable to the Puritan conscience. Like other royalist Puritans, neither Spurstowe nor Hampden were against the king's person—they never condoned the king's execution. This loyalty to the king, evident in the early 1640s, was somewhat dashed when Hampden met an early death in 1643. Several scholars have speculated the course of British history had Hampden lived longer; the discussion is mute, however, as Hampden did die in 1643, ushering in a procession of events that would culminate in the king's trial.

Tension had existed between the Anglicans and Presbyterians since the times of Thomas Cartwright, and again became acute in the 1630's. Edward Bagshaw, Sr., as a lawyer, had attacked the political rights of the bishops, and consequently was silenced. At Archbishop Laud's desire, and with his assistance, Bishop Joseph Hall, then of Exeter, defended the Episcopate's sacred claims in *Episcopacy by Divine Right Asserted* (1640); it was followed the next year with *An Humble Remonstrance to* tby William Spurstoweeloquent and continued defense of divine-right Episcopacy. The Presbyterian response, entitled, *An Answer to a Book Entitled A Humble Remonstrance,* was published in London in 1641 under the acronym *Smectymuus*—representing the work of five orthodox divines. Spurstowe was among the authors, the last three letters (uu, or double "u" and "s") representing his name. The other four were Stephen Marshall,

Edmund Calamy, Thomas Young, and Matthew Newcomen. On June 23, 1653, Thomas Manton conjectured on the anonymity of its authors: "I suppose the reverend authors were willing to hide under this onomastick that their work might not be received with prejudice, the faction against which they dealt, arrogating to themselves a monopoly of learning, and condemning all others as ignorants and novices not worthy to be heard."

The subtitle of the Presbyterian manuscript states its design and, possibly, the division of labor: *In which the Original of Liturgy and Episcopacy is Discussed, and Queries Propounded Concerning Both: The Parity of Bishops and Presbyters in Scripture Demonstrated, The Occasion of the Imparity in Antiquity Discovered, The Disparity of the Ancient and our Modern Bishops Manifested, The Antiquity of Ruling Elders in the Church Vindicated, and the Prelatical Church Bounded.* Popular enough to warrant at least four reprints (1654, 1660, 1661, 1680) under the name *Symectymnuus Redivivus* ("revived"), the work contributed to the ongoing debate between Episcopacy and Presbyterianism well into the late seventeenth century. Essentially, the work was one of conciliation. Denying the apostolic origin of liturgies and the divine-right of Episcopacy, its authors were willing to bear with the existence of bishops, if they were reduced to their primitive simplicity. Furthermore, they were willing to allow liturgies on the condition that certain divines reform them according to God's Word. These conditions, however, were unacceptable to the high-churchmen.

The work of *Smectymnuus* provoked Bishop Hall to respond in a brief work which, inadvertently, brought John Milton into the fore. Milton's *An Apology for Smectymnuus* (1642) was one of several attacks on the notion of divine-right Episcopacy.

In 1643 Spurstowe was chosen to attend the Westminster Assembly of Divines; he was constant in attendance, except for a brief lapse in 1645 when he was appointed Master of Catherine Hall, Cambridge, and had duties to attend there. As heir of his father's fortune, Spurstowe was a man of independent wealth; thus when the Assembly offered financial support to him on April 7, 1645, he cordially refused.

Between September and November 1648, Spurstowe was one of the clergy appointed to confer with the king in his captivity at Carisbrooke Castle on the Isle of Wight to discuss matters of importance. With the increasing divisions in Parliament between the Independents and the Presbyterians, Spurstowe was chosen to serve on the Assembly's committee to consider the Independents' grievances.

Spurstowe preached before Parliament on four occaions:

1. On July 21, 1643 he preached to a joint gathering of Lords and Commons for a special day of fasting and humiliation. John Hampden had been injured in battle and died six days later (June 18). This was a major setback for the military campaign which, at the time, was not going well. Preaching from 1 Samuel 7:6 ("And they gathered together to Mizpeh, and drew water, and poured it out before the LORD, and fasted on that day, and said there, 'We have sinned against the LORD.' And Samuel judged the children of Israel in Mizpeh."), Spurstowe entitled his sermon "England's Pattern and Duty In Its Monthly Fasts." There were two main points: (1) that true fasters should be weepers, and (2) that in fasting there should be an acknowledgment and confession of sin.

For Spurstowe this was a time of national mourning and repentance; not only did he lose a friend in John Hampden, but he feared he might lose England to popery. Fear, however, would not prevail, for there was always hope:

> To mourn and not to hope has a double evil in it, both
> in that it defiles, and in that it ruins a man. It defiles in
> that it conceives low and base thoughts of God
> Himself, in rendering our guilt more omnipotent than
> His power, and sin more hurtful than He is good; and
> it ruins in that the mind is thereby driven to a dreadful
> flight and wretched contempt of all the true means of
> recovery. But hope, which is as the cork to the net, that
> keeps it floating amidst the roughest seas, teaches a re-
> lapsed yet repenting sinner, when he despairs in him-
> self to fly to God, when he sees nothing below him,
> nothing about him, to believe there is something above
> him that can and will support. It quickens him also in
> the use of every means, and makes him to do as Mary
> did, who being above other sorrowful for the loss of
> Christ, was above all other most diligent to seek Him.

2. On November 5, 1644, the anniversary of the
Gunpowder Plot, Spurstowe preached to the House of
Lords the sermon "England's Eminent Judgments
Caused by the Abuse of God's Eminent Mercies." Based
on Ezra 9:13–14 ("And after all that is come upon us for
our evil deeds, and for our great trespass, seeing that
Thou our God hast punished us less than our iniquities
deserve, and hast given us such deliverance as this,
should we again break Thy commandments, and join
in affinity with the people of these abominations?
Wouldest not Thou be angry with us till Thou hadst
consumed us, so that there should be no remnant nor
escaping?"), Spurstowe admonished the House to show
its zeal for reformation, to suppress the monstrous
spread of popery, and, ultimately, to tend to Christ's
spiritual garden.
The anniversary was a fitting time to warn
Parliament of the danger of religious factions. Fresh in
memory were the events that took place on November

5, 1605, when a plot was discovered to blow up Parliament at its opening, with a stash of gunpowder stored in the cellars below the House of Lords. The attempt to assassinate King James I failed, but proved a perpetual reminder of the treacherous power dissents could have.

3. On June 24, 1646, Spurstowe preached to the House of Commons.

4. On August 25, 1647 he preached to the House of Lords. Apparently, these last two sermons before Parliament were never printed; only their dates are known.

On October 30, 1653, when the Independents were looking for help against the Fifth Monarchy Men (English Dissenters who believed Christ's kingdom on earth was imminent), Spurstowe preached at Paul's Cross. "The Magistrate's Dignity and Duty" was addressed to Thomas Viner, the Lord Mayor, and the Aldermen of London. Based on Psalm 82:1 ("God standeth in the congregation of the mighty; He judgeth among the gods"), Spurstowe admonished Viner to execute judgment and work righteously: "Let me beseech you to do what in you lies to keep laws, liberties, religion itself, from an irrecoverable shipwreck."

Spurstowe was among the signers of Cornelius Burgess's *A Vindication of the Ministers of the Gospel in, and about London* (1648), which opposed the anticipated trial and execution of the king. Burgess, writing on behalf of fifty-eight London ministers, said that although he (and the others) were in support of Parliament in so far that it was just, they did not support anarchy or treason. Their whole conduct, wrote Burgess, was with "loyal hearts and affection towards the king, and his posterity." Thus, many royalist Puritans supported the Parliamentary armies against the king's, but not to the hurt of the king's person, only to betterment of the king's kingdom by enabling their "dread sovereign" to free himself from the influence of corrupt bishops and prelates.

Burgess found support for his mindset in "The Solemn League and Covenant," which was ratified on May 5, 1641: "We shall, with the same sincerity, reality, and constancy, in our several vocations, endeavor, with our estates and lives, mutually to preserve the rights and privileges of the Parliaments, and the liberties of the kingdoms; and to preserve and defend the king's majesty's person and authority, in the preservation and defense of the true religion and liberties of the king-doms; that the world may bear witness with our con-sciences of our loyalty, and that we have no other thoughts or intentions to diminish his majesty's just power and greatness." Such an oath forbade the use of arms against the king's person, but demanded all law-ful means to promote true religion in the land.

Their pleas, however, were not heard. The king was executed for high treason in London on January 30, 1649. The Commons quickly issued an Act of Parliament prohibiting the proclamation of a succes-sor to Charles I. The next step in constituting the new political structure was the Act of Parliament (March 17, 1649) abolishing the office of king, effective in the Commonwealth of England and Ireland, Dominion of Wales, islands of Guernsey and Jersey, and the town of Berwick-upon-Tweed. In addition, Parliament abol-ished the House of Lords on March 19, 1649. Thus, the political power of England resided in the Parliament and the Council of State, appointed by the Commons on February 14, 1649.

Spurstowe refused the engagement of alliegiance to a government without a king or House of Lords. Consequently he was deprived of his Mastership at St. Catherine's in March 1650. The renowned Hebraist,

John Lightfoot, succeeded him. After the Restoration, Lightfoot offered to resign the Mastership in Spurstowe's favor, but he declined.

In 1654 the Spurstowes lost their only son, William, to cholera. Simeon Ashe, a close friend of the Spurstowes, preached the funeral sermon. "Christ: The Riches of the Gospel and the Hope of Christians," described William as a youth exemplary in piety: "He was like the young Timothy, knowing the Scriptures in his childhood. Though his bodily distempers did often take him off from reading in the Bible, yet he had read it twice throughout, and was the third time gotten into the New Testament, before his last sickness." Furthermore, according to Ashe, several years before death, the young Spurstowe was much affected with heaven's glory, and spoke often of the blessedness of living there forever.

As pastor of the church in Hackney, Middlesex, Spurstowe was a member of the Presbyterian 8th Classis of London along with Thomas Manton. On July 10, 1656, Spurstowe preached the funeral sermon of Lady Honor Viner, the late wife of Sir Thomas Viner. The sermon, "Death and the Grave No Bar to a Believer's Happiness," was preached in the parish church of Mary Wolnoth in Lombardstreet. Spurstowe's text, Psalm 17:15 ("I shall be satisfied when I awake with Thy likeness"), summarizes the Hackney minister's main point: "That death to the godly is no more than a sleep." Spurstowe described heaven as a glorious and majestic place: "All the joy and peace that believers are partakers of in this life is but as a drop to the ocean, as a single cluster to the whole vintage, as the thyme or honey upon the thigh of a bee to the whole hive fully fraught with it, or as the break and peep of day to the bright noontide."

From 1658–1660 Spurstowe was involved with Edward

Reynolds, Edmund Calamy, Simeon Ashe, Thomas Case, Thomas Manton, and other Presbyterian ministers in serving the Parliament of Richard Cromwell. The Parliament, however, was short lived and the conditions proved ripe for the restoration of the Stuart monarchy. Thus Spurstowe was one of several clergymen who assisted in the negotiations with Charles II in Holland on May 11, 1660. He was one of ten or twelve Presbyterians appointed Royal Chaplains, and he was one of only four of them allowed to preach at court, which they all did once. The other three were Edmund Calamy, Edward Reynolds, and Richard Baxter. Matthew Newcomen was importuned to accept the royal chaplaincy but refused. According to Baxter's *Reliquiae Baxterianae* (1696), the appointment of these Presbyterians as "chaplains in ordinary" was "for the gratifying and engaging of some chief Presbyterians," who helped to restore the Stuart monarchy.

In the discussion toward an accommodation of religious parties, Spurstowe was a commissioner to the Savoy Conference of April–July 1661. Their task was relatively simple. According to the commission, the Presbyterians were to "advise upon and review the said *Book of Common Prayer,* comparing the same with the most ancient liturgies which have been used in the church, in the primitive and purest times." The two parties, Anglicans and Presbyterians, could not come to a consensus; thus Baxter was forced to pen the Presbyterian response against the Bishops' defense of the Prayer Book. He retired to Spurstowe's house in Hackney and in eight days finished the document. Spurstowe seems to have been one of the ministers who had read and approved of the document.

At the Restoration, Charles II and his royalist Parliament took strict measures to eliminate the remaining buds of Puritanism. A new "Act of Uniformity"

(August 14, 1662) was passed that made Puritan acts of worship illegal. Those who refused to obey this law became known as "Nonconformists" or "Dissenters." Large numbers of Nonconformists went to prison because they were unwilling to give up their religious beliefs. Those who had been Anglicans before the Civil Wars were appointed to senior posts in the church. Bishops once again became members of the House of Lords. The Puritans also lost their power in politics; they would no longer be allowed to become members of the House of Commons or local counselors. They were also excluded from universities and from teaching in schools. Strict censorship was also imposed on books. All books dealing with history, science, or philosophy had to be checked by the government and the leaders of the church before they were published. Providentially, however, Charles could not dissolve the seeds of Puritanism. Several royalist Puritans were appointed to high office, where they were adept in promoting several Puritan ideals: simple piety, genuine worship, and loyalty to the Scriptures.

Unwilling to conform, Spurstowe was ejected from his Hackney pulpit, but lived near Hackney and exercised his talents in private as he had opportunity. In 1664 he visited Cambridge, and was a guest for dinner in Catherine Hall.

When the plague raged through London in 1665, Spurstowe expressed his deep sense of God's mercy, and advised his friends not to forget God's kindness. He encouraged them to act as "monitors" to one another, and to call upon one another "not to forget that God who had so eminently preserved [them]."

Not long after the plague, Spurstowe died in late January or early February 1666. He was buried in Hackney on February 8. Spurstowe founded six almshouses for six poor widows at Hackney, which were endowed by his brother, Henry Spurstowe, a London merchant. On September 30, 1668, Sarah Spurstowe married Anthony Tuckney, a colleague of Spurstowe at the Assembly.

A friend of Spurstowe's wrote: "He was a lover of good men, loving and faithful in his relations; a good child, a good father, a good husband, a good brother, a good master, a good neighbor, a good friend, a good governor, a good subject, a good minister, and all because he was a good Christian." Richard Baxter recollected the memory of several friends in the third part of his autobiography, saying of them "truly but what I know"; he called Spurstowe an "ancient, calm, reverend minister."

The Writings of William Spurstowe

Aside from the sermons already mentioned, Spurstowe published three treatises: *The Wells of Salvation* (1655), *The Spiritual Chymist* (1666), and *The Wiles of Satan* (1666). Here is an abstract of Spurstowe's work:

Based on 2 Peter 1:4 ("Whereby are given unto us exceeding great and precious promises, that by these you might be partakers of the divine nature, having escaped the corruption that is in the world through lust"), *The Wells of Salvation Opened; Or, A Treatise Discovering the Nature, Preciousness, Usefulness of Gospel-Promises, and Rules for the Right Application of Them*, was the only work of Spurstowe's reprinted (1659), and may well be the best book ever written on God's promises. In the second chapter, Spurstowe defined a promise as "a declaration of God's will." This definition permeates the whole book, and is used as the grounds of the believer's hope and comfort. It is not an arbitrary declaration of God's will, but a declaration of God's good will, says

Spurstowe. Furthermore, the promises have a particular excellency in them because Christ is the root of the promise, and the promise, in turn, is the root of faith. The things promised by God in the gospel are so sublime, excellent, and beautiful, that they surpass all other religions in worth.

Spurstowe wrote: "Faith believes the truth of those things which God has promised, and apprehends also the worth and excellency of them to be such as that thereby it is made firm and constant in its adherence, vigorous and active in its endeavors to use all means for the obtaining a conformity to God and Christ, and the escaping of the corruption that is in the world through lust." True faith, says Spurstowe, apprehends Christ in the promise; thus hope is an essential element in true faith and in the right use of the promises.

There are four ways, he says, that the promises provide comfort for believers. First, he notes the purity of the promises: "they are most pure, and free from any alloy that might debase them." Since the promises are pure, their comforts must be pure as well. Second, the comforts are full and satisfactory. The best comforts in the world cannot compare with the simplest consolation of the promises: "If we could suppose the apple of a man's eye to be as big as the body of the sun, and as piercing as the beams and heat thereof from which nothing is hid, yet among those innumerable objects that such an eye would behold, it could not spy out anything, which might be an adequate and proportional good unto the capacity of the soul," as the promises. Third, the promises are sure (whereas all other comforts are on slippery sands). No matter what condition believers find themselves in, whether prosperity or affliction, the promises remain the same. "A believer may at sometimes be drawn low, but he can never be drawn dry, while Christ is a full fountain, faith will never be an empty conduit-pipe." And <u>fourth</u>, the comforts of the promises are universal: "Such as agree with every estate, and suit every malady; they are the strong man's meat, and the sick man's cordial, the condemned sinner's pardon, and the justified person's evidence." Even the best of the world's comforts are only applicable to some people, and serve as salves for only a few sores, he writes.

Spurstowe presents ten positive rules for the right use of the promises, such as eyeing God in the promise, trusting His wisdom in their performance, and practicing the art of meditation. Considering the use of meditation, Spurstowe writes: "The bee does not derive any sweetness to the flower, but by its industry sucks the latent honey from it; so meditation conveys nothing of worth unto the promises, but it draws forth the sweetness, and discovers the beauty of it, which else without it would be little tasted or discerned." Furthermore, believers are admonished to wait on God for the realization of the promise. This waiting Spurstowe calls the "companion of all graces." The essence of the duty is not to let God wait for our obedience, but to wait as long as God sees good for His performance of the promise.

Spurstowe presents seven cautionary rules that, if followed carefully, would prevent believers from the misuse of the promises. Notable here is the distinction Spurstowe makes between providences and promises. The danger is to "build the foundation of our confidence upon [the promise] when successful, or when cross and unpleasing, to weaken the expectation of faith in the fulfilling of any good which the promise as a ground of hope holds forth to us." Thus the promises, in a sense, transcend providential events in that they are always trustworthy to the sense. One can struggle for a lifetime trying to discern whether or not a certain event had special, hidden significance, but the promises always mean what they say, and can never vary from their meaning.

Characteristic of Puritan methodology, Spurstowe addresses several cases of conscience regarding the promises. The first case deals with the issue of faith and assurance. The debate over *fides, fiducia,* and *certitude* (faith, trust, and assurance) is considered at some length. Spurstowe writes: "To keep therefore such bruised reeds from being broken, and the smoking flax from being quenched under the sense of their want of assurance, I shall by sundry demonstrations clearly show that the essence of saving faith does not stand in a prevailing assurance, that a believer may have the one and yet want the other." Contrary to some divines, Spurstowe contends that a true believer may have genuine faith and yet lack all sensible assurance. Spurstowe concludes, however, that no one should rest in having faith without assurance, or lessen their diligence in making their calling and election sure. He only acknowledges the existence of faith apart from assurance to preserve undue stress from fainting believers.

The Wells of Salvation is unique in depth and compass. Since Spurstowe considers the whole spectrum of the believer's sensible experience of the promise, it proves qualitatively better than Nicholas Byfield's *The Promises; Or, A Treatise Showing How a Godly Christian May Support His Heart with Comfort* (1619). As Spurstowe contends, the promises are for all believers in all stations of life, and not only for the spiritually downcast.

Perhaps the best quote from the book is found on page 78 of the original [this book has not been reprinted since the 17th century, but is in process for publication by Soli Deo Gloria]: "I have sometimes thought that a believer's looking upon a promise is not unlike a man's beholding of the heavens in a still and

serene evening, who when he first casts up his eye, sees
haply a star or two only to peep, and with difficulty to
put forth a feeble and disappearing light, by and by he
looks up again, and then both their number and luster
are increased, a while after he views the heavens again,
and then the whole firmament, from every quarter, with
a numberless multitude of stars, is richly enameled, as
with so many golden studs."

In *The Spiritual Chymist; Or, Six Decades of Divine
Mediations on Several Subjects,* Spurstowe shows conso-
nance with the Puritan meditative tradition by making
spiritual use of ordinary objects. The text on the title
page provides the work's tone: "My meditation of Him
shall be sweet" (Psalm 104:34).

Spurstowe reflects on celestial and terrestrial things;
among his meditations are thoughts on the Milky Way,
time and eternity, a mote in the eye, the morning dew,
a pearl, a lamp, a prison, a candlestick, a pepper-corn, a
rock, the Bible, spiritual warfare, banishment, con-
tentment, and natural heat. Published posthumously,
Spurstowe was unable to finalize the manuscript before
the press; but even with the somewhat spotted sentences, the meditations are no less engaging than
Bishop Hall's Contemplations.

Here is Spurstowe's fourth meditation, "Upon a
Picture and a Statue":

> In what a differing manner is the image and representa-
> tion of the same person brought into these two pieces
> of art? In the one it is effected by the soft and silent
> touches of the pencil, which happily convey the like-
> ness and beauty together. In the other it is formed by
> the rough and loud strokes of the hammer, and by the
> deep cutting and sculptures of instruments of steel. In
> as strange and far differing way is the heavenly image of
> God formed in the souls of new converts, when first
> made partakers of the divine nature. In some God

paints (if I may so speak) His own likeness by a still
and calm delineation of it upon the table of their
hearts. In others He carves it by afflicting them with a
great measure of terrors, and wounding their souls with
a thorough sense both of the guilt and defilement of
sin. But in this diversity of working, God is no way ne-
cessitated or limited by the disposition and temper of
the matter, as other artists are, but is freely guided by
the counsel of His own will, which is the sole rule and
measure of all His actions towards the creature, as His
Word is of theirs towards Him. Lord, therefore do with
me what Thou please. Let me be but Thine, and I will
not prescribe Thy wisdom the way to make me Thine;
bruise, break, wound, yea, kill, Lord, so that I may be
made alive again by Thy power and bear Thy holy image, according to which I was first made, and to which
by Thy grace and might only I can be restored.

Published posthumously in 1666, *Satana Nohmata; Or,
The Wiles of Satan in a Discourse upon 2 Corinthians 2:11*
(here reprinted), is the compilation of several notes on
Satan's devices. Spurstowe was in the arduous task of
compiling, editing, and expanding *The Wiles* when his
conflict with the world ended. He had progressed to
the sixth section of the fourth chapter. The remaining
work is largely in note form, collected from his papers.

Spurstowe wrote *The Wiles* to discover Satan's art and
policy, to unmask and bring the great deceiver into the
open, so that his readers, being forewarned, might be
forearmed. Much thought was given on the subject, as
is evident from sections in *The Wells of Salvation* (see
chapter 18, "Four differences between the promises of
God and Satan") and *The Spiritual Chymist* (see the 58th
meditation, "Upon the Spiritual Warfare"). Spurstowe
desired to dissolve the works of the devil, and sent the
book to the press because he saw the necessity of the
times demanded it. Too many professing Christians
were caught up in strife and division—the cunning

craft of Satan's tactic.

The thesis of *The Wiles* is that "Satan is full of devices, and studies arts of circumvention, by which he unweariedly seeks the irrecoverable ruin of the souls of men." Throughout the work Spurstowe uncovers Satan's ability to tempt, Satan's wiles, and the antidotes to preserve against such temptations. The work is sound, informative, and relevant to western society, where interest in spiritual matters has increased in recent years. Though not as detailed as Richard Gilpin's *A Treatise of Satan's Temptations* [reprinted by Soli Deo Gloria], nor as exhaustive as John Downame's *The Christian's Warfare*, Spurstowe's little book is every bit as helpful. It can be argued that Spurstowe's insight surpassed both Gilpin's and Downame's, as the discourse was the culmination of his life's experience, finalized on the borders of eternity.

Do you want to be aware of Satan's devices in your life? Do you want to know how to stand fast and resist him? Read Spurstowe's treatise with care and diligence; ponder, reflect, and remember, for "Satan is always tempting, he has always fiery darts about him, though he does not throw them; he is always biting at the heal, therefore be always ready to make resistance."

Randall Pederson
Grand Rapids, Michigan
July 2003

Chapter 1

An Introduction to the Words

Seldom or never do judges become advocates; they give sentence on the crime, but they never plead the cause of the offender. In doing the one, they discharge the most solemn duty of their place, but in undertaking the other they descend, as it were, from the throne to the bar and go both below themselves and besides the rule. A pleading judge is no well-tuned cymbal. And yet, if we look into these two epistles of Paul to the Corinthians, we shall find him excerising both these distinct offices towards the same person in one and the same cause.

In the first we may behold Him as a just and severe judge, drawing forth the spiritual sword of the Church, and smiting with it the incestuous person, in as great a height of zeal as Samuel did Agag, to cutting him off from all communion with that body of which he was a member. He was the first (as Calvin expressed it) who stained the beauty of that church with so foul a sin and scandal. If we turn our eyes to our text, we see the same apostle performing the office of a most compassionate advocate in pleading the cause of him to the Corinthians who, by his command, was cut off and cast out from among them. He who was the subject of his censure as a judge is now the object of his entreaties as an advocate. And the arguments which he uses for his reception into the bosom of their love are not more numerous than weighty.

A brief view of some of these will not be impertinent, in that they lead us in an orderly way unto the

1

text, which is the last, but not the least of those many persuasive pleas which he urges on his behalf.

The first plea is drawn from the law of equity, which is, as Philo calls it, the nurse of justice: "Sufficient to such a man is the punishment which was inflicted of many" (verse 6). Though rewards and punishments are the golden hinges upon which the welfare of every state turns, yet are they to be regulated by a just and fit measure. No censures are to be excessive, much less church censures, whose end is chiefly medicinal. They are (as Augustine says of the corrections of God) chastisements to procure amendment, not to work ruin.

A second plea is from the present danger: "Lest perhaps such an one should be swallowed up with overmuch sorrow" (verse 7).

Inward troubles and perplexities of mind are far more corrosive and wasting than outward ones. The wheels of a clock, whose motion is strong, wears sooner than the finger which moves gently without. They are oftentimes like a tempestuous and angry sea which not only tosses the ship, but sinks it. And it does not become sailors to be spectators of any man's ruin without casting forth some cord or plank, by the help of which he might reach the shore. It is Job's censure of him who did not show pity to the afflicted, that he had forsaken the fear of the Almighty (Job 6:14).

A third plea is that he might have some proof whether they are "obedient in all things" (verse 9). Spiritual fathers, as well as natural ones, delight in the reiterated acts of their childrens' obedience as being the most legible characteristics of a son-like disposition. And therefore the apostle, who had only a single trial of their willing compliance to his commands, seeks the confirmation of it by a second testimony: that as they had shown themselves forward in putting away from among them that person whose sin was not to be

paralleled among the heathen, so now they would, at
his entreaties, show the like readiness in the readmis-
sion of him into their love and favor who, of a presumptuous sinner, had become a humble and broken
penitent.

4 A fourth plea is from his own practice. He had for
their sakes forgiven him, as in the sight or person of
Christ (verse 10). That is, as he first awakened them to
judge the sin with which for a time they were not affected, so now, by his example, in his sincere pardon-
ing of it, as in Christ's sight, he induced them to do the
same, and also teach them how to temper their zeal
aright in being neither too remiss in using the censures of the Church nor too rigorous in retaining them
when inflicted. Both extremes would be equally preju-
dicial to the beauty of their zeal. It is just so with the
blood in the body, which, if it be diluted through
phlegm, or too fiery through choler, makes the complexion too wane and sallow, or too red and high col-
ored.

5 A fifth plea is that which comes under present consideration, and is to be insisted on as the subject of this
present discourse: "lest Satan should get an advantage
of us." In this verse there are two principal parts, which
equally divide and share the verse between them:

First, there is a useful caution of circumspection:
"lest Satan should get an advantage." The general con-
cernment of this is implied in the relative particle "us."
For in this matter Satan, as a common adversary, en-
deavored more than a single supplantation; he did not
bait a hook, but spread a net. For should the incestuous
person through despair miscarry, it might occasion a
rent between the apostle and the Corinthians that
would be difficult to make up. It might render the
gospel less amiable to those upon whom it had newly
dawned, and cause it to be as unwelcome and offensive,

as light is to weak and sore eyes. It might blemish the censures of the church as having too deep a tincture of pharisaic rigor, and having their whole power tending to destruction rather than to edification.

Therefore the apostle, like a wise physician, is more than ordinarily anxious that the patient does not die under their hands, and Satan get the advantage of them by both his sin and sorrow.

The words in the original are diversly expounded by various interpreters. The Vulgate reads it, "that we be not circumvented by Satan." Like a cunning wrestler or fencer, Satan is various and uncertain in his motions so that he may take the better hold, or strike his adversary with a greater advantage. Beza renders it thus: "that Satan does not get by far the better of us," not by open force, but by unforeseen artifices and slights. Erasmus interprets it: "lest Satan should usurp upon us." That is, lest he who has nothing by right should, by fraud obtain a kind of possession among us by snatching and taking him from us as his own who is a member of our body. The entire union of the body we ought to preserve from such ruptures and avulsions by the due tempering of our zeal and charity towards those who, by the strength of temptation, fall into sin, and who, by their deep sorrow, testify their unfeigned repentance for sin.

Others conceive it to be a metaphor taken from avaricious and greedy persons who, for gain's sake in their contracts and bargains, by guile and fraud, overreach those whom they deal with. In all these expositions there is so full a concurrence and agreement to the circumstances of the place and the practices of Satan that I shall not, by giving a preeminence to any one above the other, determine the judgment of the intelligent reader which to take, but wholly leave him to his free choice. I shall only intimate that my translation favors the last one.

Second, there is the forcible and prevailing motive to stir up their circumspection: "for we are not ignorant of his devices." The Greek word for devices, in its general acceptance, signifies the thoughts and musings of the mind (as Estius observes); but in a more strict and confined sense it is applied to such thoughts that are on purpose framed to deceive, and by studied artifices to bring about designed ends in any kind whatsoever. Such are ambushes in war, fakes in wrestling, deceits in gaming, policies in state, fallacies in disputing, and dark and covered sentences in rhetoric, in which one thing is spoken and another intended.

Therefore the apostle said that he was not ignorant of Satan's "cogitations," as the Vulgate and other translations also render the words. It is not to be understood of any intuitive power and ability which he assumed to himself of discerning and prying into the most retired thoughts of the prince of darkness—which are only open and naked to the eye of God, whose sacred royalty it is to search the hearts both of men and angels—but of a practical and experimental knowledge, which he and other believers also attain to by a diligent observance of their ways and actions. In these actions they reveal the mysterious arts and snares of the tempter, spread like the nets of a cunning fowler, to trap them in every motion and step that they make, not only by his various allurements to sin, but also by his perverting their best duties, so as to make them to be losers thereby, and himself to be the only gainer. And this was it in which Satan sought to get the better of the Corinthians, turning their just zeal against the sin of the incestuous person into an inexorable severity against his repentance, though he was well nigh swallowed up by sorrow.

Chapter 2

The Main Proposition of the Discourse

I may perhaps have lingered too long upon the borders of the text, and may have spun out the explication of a few words into too long a thread. But my purpose was only to free the words from any difficulty which might seem to sit upon them, like dark shadows on the top of the mountain, or mists in the valley, that intercept the light. I think that they are like a bright and unspotted mirror which exactly presents the object or species that is shed upon it to the eye of every beholder.

So clearly do they hold forth this one proposition, in which both parts of the verse, the caution of circumspection given, and the ground or motive to it, equally center.

PROPOSITION: Satan is full of devices, and studies arts of circumvention by which he unweariedly seeks the irrecoverable ruin of the souls of men.

It is the observation of the learned Zanchius that Satan has more than twenty distinct names and appellations given to him in the Scripture. Some of them set forth the high impurity of his nature, in opposition to that state of holiness in which the blessed angels stand, and from which he is fallen. In this respect he is called an unclean spirit in Mark 9:25, a spirit of wickedness in Ephesians 6:12, and the evil one in Matthew 13:19. Other of his titles speak of the sovereignty and dominion which he exercises over multitudes of men, and hence he is called by our Savior the prince of this world in John 12:31. The apostle calls him the god of this world in 2 Corinthians 4:4.

Some of his other titles point to his malice and fierce rage, armed with power; hence he is called the accuser of the brethren in Revelation 12:10; a roaring lion, not seeking whom he may bite, but whom he may devour, in 1 Peter 5:8; a great red dragon, that out of his mouth sends forth waters, in Revelation 12:15, and who, with his tail, casts down the third part of the stars of heaven to the earth, in Revelation 12:4.

Others names declare his craft to deceive, his wiles to ensnare, and his dexterity and skill to tempt. In this regard he is said to be the father of lies in John 8:44; the old serpent that, by his windings and turnings, deceives all the world, in Revelation 12:9; and the tempter in Matthew 4:3. This name some think to be so peculiar to the devil, since it agrees to no other person or thing. Though men tempt instrumentally and the world materially, yet efficiently Satan only is said to tempt.

But among the many ways by which Holy Writ signalizes the transcendent enmity that the devil bears to the church and chosen of God, there are none more to be eyed or dreaded than his pernicious wiles and devices. He captivates more by his hidden snares than he wounds by his fiery darts. He poisons more as a hissing serpent than he devours as a roaring lion. He cheats more as a tempter than he hurts as an accuser. And as he in his immediate workings has always been (and still is) more mischievous to the church and truth of God by his machinations and arts than by his open force, so likewise have those instruments and emissaries of his in the succession of all ages proven more fatal to the welfare of religion that have rather used the head of this serpent than the paw of this lion; and have carried on their designs by fraud and subtlety rather than by a hostile war and defiance.

The Midianites vexed Israel more by their wiles (Numbers 25:18) than the combined powers of all the

kings of Canaan did by frequent battles. The Samaritan
faction obstructed the building of the temple by false
insinuations (Ezra 4:6), by scornful derisions (Nehemi-
ah 4:3), and by pretended compliances of building with
Zerubbabel, and the chief of the fathers (Ezra 4:2).
Julian the infamous apostate more endangered the
gospel, and lessened the number of its professors, by
his serpentine policies than all his predecessors had
done by their bloody persecutions, as Augustine and
other of the ancients have truly observed. Yea, and
Romish Babylon itself, though it has exceeded in
cruelty all the Edomites of the former ages, in making
her garments red, and her self drunk, with the blood of
the saints as with new wine, yet the advancement of the
papacy has been accompanied, after the working of
Satan, with all power, signs, and lying wonders, and
with all deceivableness of unrighteousness (2 Thessalonians 2:9–10); in feigning apparitions of angels and
spirits, in forging of decrees of counsels and corrupting of fathers, in resembling and dissembling of piety,
in swearing and forswearing, in fawnings, flatterings,
bribings, and the use of all arts of deceit and imposture
that wickedness itself can devise or exercise.

    If then it is a study and labor not unusual to the mil-
itary profession to record the stratagems of the most
renowned chieftains in war, as Vegetius, Frontinus, and
others have done; to treat the ordering of armies and
ranging them into several forms and figures, as Aelian
in his *Tactics* has done; or to write with Lypsius of the
warlike engines and weapons of the ancients—it cannot but be both grateful and necessary to acquaint such
who are engaged in a spiritual warfare against Satan
and his infernal legions as what his methods of temptation, his arts of loose skirmishing, and close fighting
are with those against whom he sets the battle in array;
what the ways of his retreats and feigned flying are, so

that they may neither be ensnared by his wiles, nor vanquished by his power. To this end therefore, in the pursuance of that needful truth which I have propounded to insist on, I shall endeavor to expound the following particulars. I intend:

1. To demonstrate the great abilities of Satan as a tempter, to effect and bring about his cursed designs in making his suggestions to become our sins, his snares our chains, his bait our food, his will our rule, and his inventions our circumventions.

2. To set down not by way of enumeration, but by example, some of those grand stratagems and usual polices which too often render him the conqueror and us the captives. For, as Jerome said, he who has a multitude of distinct names also has as many arts to hurt and destroy.

3. To furnish the combatants in this war and conflict with weapons out of the Tower of David (Song of Solomon 4:4), the armory of the Holy Scripture, such, which being mighty through God, may both pierce the scales of this hellish leviathan, though shut up together as with a close seal (Job 41:15) and may also safeguard them against the sore danger of his poisonous and fiery arrows.

Chapter 3

The Great Ability of Satan to Tempt

I shall offer the following six demonstrations to evidence the great ability of Satan to tempt. Ever since he left his own station, he has never ceased to malign ours, and has become by both office and practice a tempter so that he might draw man from his happiness into the same irreparable and cursed condition as himself.

DEMONSTRATION 1. In his nature, he is both a spiritual and an intellectual essence, in each of which respects his advantage over man is very great, who in the most refined, and supreme part of his being falls as far short of an angel as a small glittering spark does a fair and well-polished diamond, or as a twinkling star does of a refulgent sun. An angel, said Bellarmine, is a most perfect and spiritual substance. But the soul is a spirit imperfectly and by halves; it has the form of an earthly body and part of a man, who is a middle kind of creature, and has something in common with angels above him and with beasts which are below him.

As a spirit, therefore, Satan can convey himself and his suggestions to both the understanding and the will in a more intimate and efficacious manner than any human agent possibly can. For when one man becomes a tempter to another, he uses the mediation of the outward senses to which he can only apply and communicate the object; but he cannot by any physical or natural power gain an immediate access to the internal faculties of the soul and lodge the temptation, as Joseph's steward hid the cup in Benjamin's sack without his knowledge. But such is the power of this infernal angel that, though he is totally barred from all kinds of intercourse with the immediate and immanent operations of the reasonable soul, and can no more look into the thoughts and musings of the heart than a common eye can pry into the bowels of the earth and describe those numerous conceptions with which it travels in its womb, yet he can as easily get into the fancy, which is next to that mysterious chamber of the soul, which to God alone is all light, and to every created power all darkness, as any man can enter into a room that is possessed of a key that gives him free admittance. And he can make use of all those species and signatures of things that are lodged in it, disposing and ordering them as a painter does his many colors, that lie confusedly before him in their various shades to express the portraiture and image of that person whom he would delineate by them. He can both continue and reiterate the presentation of the objects which he offers to the fancy as often and as long as it pleases him.

Now, how much such a power (when permitted by God) can further a compliance in the soul to all those suggestions which the "father of lies" secretly instills we may easily conjecture if we do but a little consider what the natural use of the fancy is to both the understanding and the will. To the understanding, it is a prompt assistant in matter of invention to supply it with a variety of objects whereon to work; and from the quickness of its operation the multiplicity, levity, and volubility of the thoughts chiefly arise which, when they become excessive through an undue and over-hasty obtrusion of the species, are to be deemed in both natural and moral things as a disease and distemper of the faculty rather than a power or perfection; in regard that the worth of some objects justly requires an immolation and fixed stay of the thoughts upon them. To

the will, its office is to elicit and excite its desires towards some convenient and pleasing object in which
for the most part it is so successful that often times
plausible fancies do more take and sway with the will
than knotty and severe arguments. There is a natural
aptness in men to be moved by such inducements as
carry in them more beauty to entice than force of reason to compel; the freedom of the will being seemingly
less infringed in the one than in the other. Therefore
Satan, by reason of the spirituality of his being, can
have such a free access unto the fancy, and can improve
all the images and representations of things that are in
it, to insinuate himself and his serpentine suggestions
to both the understanding and will, so inwardly that he
is said to put it into the heart of Judas to betray Christ
(John 13:2), to fill the heart of Ananias to lie to the
Holy Ghost (Acts 5:3). So powerful is he that the
Scripture uses the same word to express the working of
Satan in the children of disobedience (Ephesians 2:3)
by which it sets forth the efficacious and powerful
working of God in believers (Philippians 2:13). How
can it otherwise be but that he must be a powerful and
prevailing adversary? Yet this difference must be put between the operations of the one and the other, that the
Spirit of God works by divine infusions of grace, which
effectually sway the soul to an assent or consent, Satan
only by moral persuasions, which may be powerful to
solicit, but not to constrain. And in this respect he is
(as Jerome truly calls him) a feeble and weak enemy,
who can only overcome him who yields, not him who
resists; and hurts him who puts his weapons into his
hand, not him who keeps them in his own.

Second, as Satan is a spiritual being, he is also an
intellectual being. And by the same law of creation by
which he excels man in the one, he far outstrips him in
the other. Now, in the understanding of Adam there

was such an inbred force and power that when God brought all the creatures to him as their Lord to see what he would name them (Genesis 2:19). In giving the creatures their names, Adam characterized their nature; he did not give it to them at random (as the Socinians wickedly imagine, who make him little above the stature of a child in knowledge). That being true, how much more must the angelic nature be endowed with innate and implanted species of things, that are more universal and extensive unto several objects, it being the most supreme in the hierachy of intelligent creatures, for whose sake all natural objects were made that they might be known and discerned by them. True, Satan, by his voluntary defection from God, has lost that glorious robe of holiness that made him a peer of heaven, and dignified him with the title of a son of God. He has also (I conceive) impaired his natural abilities, so that he has become in power, wisdom, and knowledge inferior to those glorious inhabitants of the sacred palace, who have kept their first estate, and not departed from that purity that is as ancient as their being. For why should not the sin of angels operate as strongly upon them as the lapse and disobedience of man did upon him, whose spiritual parts were thereby wholly destroyed, and his natural parts sorely maimed. But though his fall has debased his being, yet it has not totally changed it; he still has the nature, though not the perfection, of an angel. And though he is inferior to them whose equal originally he was in all kind of endowments, yet he still retains so great a superiority over the elementary, sensitive, and intellectual part of the world that he is not only dreaded for his power, which sometimes he puts forth in wonderful effects; but is also adored for his wisdom and knowledge as a god by many nations.

It is observable that Beelzebub, in 2 Kings 1:2, is

called "the god of Ekron," and in Luke 11:15 is termed "the prince of devils." In the kingdom of sin and darkness he is a god, but in the kingdom of grace he is a devil, and more ghastly than hell itself by his sinful deformity; and though he seldom or never appears in that dress, but palliates and gilds his suggestions—they sometime seem to be rather lapses from heaven than smoke rising from the bottomless pit, and to savor more of angelical purity than diabolical filthiness—yet is he not therefore to be any less observed by us. We ought rather to be all the more watchful since we have such a serpent to deal with that can hide his deadly poison with a beautiful and shining skin. And if the ancient church, while Augustine was a Manichean, and a busy wrangler against them was wont to pray, "Lord, deliver us from Augustine's subtlety and reasonings," how much more have believers need to make the same prayer, and often to reiterate it, "Lord, deliver us from the arts and fallacies of Satan," whose malice is great, whose abilities are matchless, and which transcend the line of human wisdom, when drawn out to the utmost period of its extension.

But as the measure of his knowledge is more full and ample, so the manner of his knowledge and apprehending objects is more noble and perfect than the way by which man comes to the knowledge of things that are before him. The scholastics, who abound with many intemperate niceties and curious disputes about the understanding of angels (in which they justly incur the rebuke of the apostle in Colossians 2:18 of intruding into those things which they have not seen), though in other particulars they are not a little divided, yet in this position their consent in general is that angels are beings that are full of knowledge, but not such as exercise a plurality of intellect in reasoning and argumentation as we do, whose knowledge is much built upon deductions and consequences, that are derived from confessed principles. They grant angels' knowledge not to be simultaneous, but successive, so that they know one object after another; but it has no dependence so as to know one thing by or from another, but by one single view or intuition they fully discern the object that is before them, as a man does the face of a friend as soon as he beholds him, without the least hesitance or inquiry who he is.

Now if we should take for granted that the knowledge of angels is this exact, and that at first sight the same object is better understood by them than it can be by the many and most pregnant conceptions of the human intellect, it must evidence the abilities of Satan in tempting to be such that man cannot but be as unfit an adversary to maintain a dispute against him as the young infant would have been to have resisted the sword which Solomon called for to divide it between the two harlots. But I shall not need to wind up the knowledge of angels to so high a key of perfection, or to abet the common opinion of the schoolmen, to make it any part of the basis or proof in demonstrating the power of the devil as a tempter. For I conceive with Cameron and others that their knowledge is arguitive (as he terms it) and not intuitive, and that they do reason from the effect to the cause, from the sign to the event, as is apparent in those conjectures that they make about the thoughts of men, which no angel, either good or bad, can otherwise discover than by some commotion which they cause externally in the body or internally in the passions. Only such is the marvelous quickness and agility of their conceptions that their intellectual motions are in respect of ours as the motion of the sun in the heavens is to the motion of the shadow on the dial, like the swift flight of an eagle is to the creeping of a snail, or the readiness of an expert mathematician is to a slow and unskillful accountant who can in fewer minutes resolve that which you demand of him than the other can in many hours or days. And this vast imparity which is between the angelic and human understanding is enough to make good this first demonstration of Satan's ability to tempt, as he is both a spiritual and intellectual essence.

DEMONSTRATION 2. The second demonstration which aptly confirms the same truth with the former is from the duration and long experience of the devil, who has thereby become skillful to destroy, and to have his temptations be like the arrows of a mighty expert man, none of which return in vain (Jeremiah 50:9). In Scripture, as he is for his natural endowments often called a knowing or intelligent one, so he is for his acquired subtlety called an old serpent (Revelation 12:9), having been well nigh as long a tempter, nay, a murderer, as he has been an angel. He must therefore—by the many revolutions and successive generations of men, in which he has not been an idle spectator, but a busy actor—be more versed in this art and mystery of wickedness than he was in the non-age and infancy of his being when he first clothed himself in the shape of a serpent. For it is proper only to God, to whose knowledge all things are present, at all times, and before all times, not to be taught by experience. But there is no creature so perfect in its knowledge but it may and does learn something for the time present and to come by the times which are past.

Experience is like the honey that Jonathan tasted, which enlightened his eyes, and made him more fit for action than he was before. It begets an aptitude for the managing of such affairs which youth can no more undergo than David could the armor of Saul which he had not tried. Who is more fit to minister medicine to a weak and infirmed patient than an ancient and well-practiced physician? Who is more able to treat a wounded spirit, and to ease a troubled conscience, than a holy and experienced divine? Who may be better trusted to sit at the helm of a state than such persons whom years have made both venerable and prudent? It was the rash advice of Rehoboam's young counselors that well nigh lost him his crown, and occasioned the ten tribes to fall off from the house of David, and to form themselves into a distinct kingdom (1 Kings 12:20). They seemed in their counsels to exercise more mettle and courage than the old men who stood before Solomon, his father, but the other displayed more wisdom.

New liquor works and stirs more in the cask than older, but yet is as unfit to be drawn as their counsel was to be followed. It was also the unfit choice of persons in the Council of Arimine, deputed by the orthodox unto the Emperor, that much injured the truth. They sent young men who were little learned, and as little cautious in the weighty affairs of religion, with which they were entrusted. The Arians sent an equal number of their faction, who were aged and crafty men, well furnished with wit and learning, whereby they easily prevailed against them. And what other issue could be expected when unskillful novices were to take up their toy swords against ancient and cunning masters of the art of fencing? It is multitudes of years that teaches wisdom (said Elihu in Job 32:7), and produces those mature fruits which youth, that is like a plant not well rooted, is unable to bear. Homer, who extolled Nestor as an oracle of wisdom, as a fountain of fluency and sweetness of speech, yet withal makes him as wonderful for his age as peerless for his perfection. Josephus also attributes the art of astronomy to the patriarchs of the first age, who taught their posterity the motions of the heavens and the courses of the stars by

certain monuments and pillars in which they had set
down the observations, which themselves had experienced in those many centuries of years to which the life
of man was then extended. One end (as some have
deemed) of God's giving them so long a time above
others, that they might be the authors of this science
unto later ages which otherwise, after that great con-
traction of man's life by God Himself, would hardly, if
at all, have been attained to. If then time and experience are so requisite to knowledge and wisdom that it
is in some things the genuine parent of it, and in other
things the great improver of it, how much then must
five thousand years' experience enable Satan to tempt,
who has all his time been as diligent an observer of
men as he has been an adversary against them? How
skillful must he be in his black and accursed art who
has compiled his temptations into systems, which he
has in readiness by him, and does with much art continually make use of, being one that does not know in
the least what it is either to forget or grow old.
Sublunary beings, though they do from time receive a
maturity and perfection, yet it is not extended in a parallel line with their duration; as they have a time of
beauty and strength, so also they have an age of deformity and weakness, and by their long sitting under the
deathful shades of the wings of time are at last wasted
and worn out. But Satan feels none of time's powerful
impressions; time has rather added to him than taken
away from him, multiplying continually those experi-
ences which increase his subtlety and advantage in
tempting, as I shall show in three particulars:

• First, his long experience as a tempter has made
him exact in discerning and choosing the most fitting
seasons for it, the right timing of which has a powerful
and effective influence into all kinds of enterprises
whatever. Upon whose sword does victory most con-

stantly build its triumph than his who is most diligent in spying out or improving advantages against his enemy? Whose entreaties and persuasions do with sweetness more allure, and with mildness overcome, the harshness and severity of some men's temper than his who observes the softest and most calm seasons of speech? Whose husbandry is crowned with a more successful harvest than his who is most prudent and circumspect about the seed time? Opportunity is the joint of time, and he who wisely can hit it is never disappointed in his aims. One blow on the iron, as it comes glowing and sparkling from the forge, more easily bows and fashions it than many repeated strokes when it is returned to its natural coldness. One timely pull more facilitates the ringing of the bell than many unskilful and laborious tugs on the rope.

Now, as there are none as watchful as Satan to spy out any advantages, so there are none as knowing to discern the very nick of time when the temptation will be more prevalent. Man often miscarries, and his undertakings become like immature births, because he does not know his time (Ecclesiastes 9:12). But Satan is more successful in his undertakings because he acts from experience, and fully understands when and how to apply himself to every age and constitution. All his methods of temptation are like the aphorisms of physicians, which are nothing but the collections of experimental observations drawn into rules to direct and order their practice by. And as Galen makes the two legs upon which the whole body of medicine stands to be reason and experience, so may I say that the two chief parts in which the art of the devil's subtlety in tempting consists are the greatness of his natural knowledge and the length of his experience.

• Second, his experience, which now amounts to about five thousand years, gives him great advantage in

tempting, as it makes him dexterous and ready in the
obviating of difficulties, and replying to every doubt
that is made when any suggestion is propounded and
urged by him. Satan can with great skill palliate and
disguise the deformity of sin by giving it a false complexion, by drawing a veil over it, or by showing it half-
faced (as Apelles painted King Antigonus to conceal
the want of his eye). Yet there are but few temptations
to scandalous and gross sins but at first startle the consciences of natural men, much more of others, and
raise a cloud of objections which must be scattered before their consent can be gained. Now the objections
or doubts which arise in mens' minds of this present
age are no other than what Satan has again and again
met with in every generation and succession of men,
yea, almost in every person, when tempted by him to
the same or like sin. And as he still expects for the future to find the same reasonings to hinder and keep off
a compliance with his suggestions, so what replies or
answers he has experienced to be most prevalent, either
for perverting the knowledge or staggering the faith of
the tempted, them he still makes use of from time to
time to remove the same prejudices that stir in others
when set upon by him to commit the same sin. And
this it is which often times startles and perplexes many
Christians, not only that they are tempted to sin, but
that their pleas and arguments against it are so suddenly answered and replied unto. No sooner can they
give an objection but the old serpent has a solution;
and like a subtle sophister he always has something to
return to whatever they can object. But if they considered that the evils to which they are tempted are no
other than what has been suggested unto thousands, so
their arguments brought against them are no other
than what he has been thousands of times acquainted
with and replied unto, they would not so much wonder

at his nimbleness in this kind, nor take the way of arguing as most convenient to oppose him. Christ's rebuke, "Get thee hence, Satan" (Matthew 4:10), did more to foil him than all reasonings and authorities produced. And the safest way for us to come off clear with him is rather to be resolute in a flat denial than busy in an eager dispute. When Naomi saw that Ruth was steadfastly minded to go with her, she stopped speaking to her (Ruth 1:18).

• Third, his experience animates him with confidence to assault the best and holiest of saints; if not to extinguish their light, yet to eclipse their luster; if not to cause a shipwreck, yet to raise a storm; if not to hinder their happy end, yet to molest them in their way. Such practices he has found not only to have some success against the strong, but to intimidate and discourage the weak, who are apt from the particular foils of renowned Christians in the faith, to make sad conclusions against themselves and cry out, "What shall the spats and rafters do if the pillars of the building tremble? What shall the reeds and willows do if the cedars are shaken?" Who has wrestled with him and not halted? Who has entered the field against him and not been wounded by him? Was not Noah a just and perfect man, one who walked with God when all flesh had corrupted their way, smitten with the darts of this Apollyon between the joints and the harness? Was not Lot, whose righteous soul was vexed from day to day with the unlawful deeds of Sodom, enticed by his arts into the complicated lusts of drunkenness and incest? Was not David (a man after God's own heart) a sad instance of both his power and man's frailty? Through Satan's instigation, David made a second crime to be the consequence of a former one; and to cover the deformity of his adultery, he sent Uriah drunk to his bed; and then he became a murderer when that would not do, and

dispatched him to his grave? How then shall I, who fall
as far short of them as a winter's day does a summer's
day, who have neither that life, heat, or heavenly influ-
ences with which they were filled, be ever able to stand?
But yet, as no man ought to presume that there are any
degrees of grace that will exempt him from Satan's on-
sets, who is not afraid to war with Michael and his
Angels (Revelation 12:7), much less with the woman
and her seed, so none ought to despair by reason of the
weakness of his grace of maintaining a conflict with
him because, though his rage has been great and his
strategies many, yet he has he never been able to make
the seed of grace, in its conception, to prove abortive,
nor has he ever been able to destroy a believer in his
swaddling-bands, much less in his armor.

DEMONSTRATION 3. A third demonstration which
may further evidence the abilities of Satan in tempting
is that it is the only design and business that he has
propounded unto himself, and has prosecuted with
most unwearied diligence ever since he became an
impure devil instead of a holy angel.

It is the grand and sole business in which he lays
himself out, and thereby becomes not only more dexterous in it, but also more formidable. It is an Italian
Proverb: "Lord, deliver me from a man who has but one
business to do." That man will be sure to mind and
tend it, and thereby get many advantages against an
encumbered adversary who can never obtain the least
against him. For it is with the powers and faculties of
rational beings as it is with other things which become
more or less active and vigorous, according to the
combination or division which they undergo. Many
small wax lights, which of themselves burn faintly,
when put into one torch or taper, send forth a bright
and shining flame; many little bells, which tinkle together to please children, when melted and cast into

one great bell, affect the ear with a more solemn and awful sound; many single threads, which snap asunder with the least touch, when twisted together make a strong cable which can withstand the fury and violence of a storm.

So it is with the mind: the more it is scattered and divided through multiplicity of objects, the more weak it is; and the more it is fixed on one single object, the more masculine and strong are the operations of it, either for good or for evil. Therefore David, who desired to excel in holiness, made it his prayer in Psalm 86:11 that God would unite his heart to fear His name. Jerome reads it, "Make my heart one," that is, "Incline it only to Thy fear," implying thereby that divided interests in the heart both distract and weaken it. When the Scripture likewise would set forth the awful depravation of man's estate, it says that every imagination of his heart was only evil continually (Genesis 6:5). There is not the least contrary principle to check or to restrain those ebullitions of lust which flow and ascend from the heart, as water from a fountain or sparks from a furnace.

Now thus it is with Satan: he is wholly bent to evil, and makes it his only study to dive and search into men so that he may better fasten his temptations upon them. It is the question which God puts to him in Job 1:8: "Hast thou considered My servant Job?" or as the Septuagint renders it, "Hast thou attended with thy mind My servant Job?" What is implied is that his practice and end is in going to and fro in the earth; he does not travel it as a pilgrim, but as a spy who closely observes every person and thing as he passes along. He does not go forward a step without noting every man's estate, temper, age, calling, and company so that he may with greater advantage tempt to evil, and thereby bring men into the same misery and condemnation as himself. And indeed, whosoever duly weighs the perfect antipathy that is in Satan, unto both God and holiness, can hardly conceive in what other thing he should exercise himself than to tempt and solicit men to sin. For such is the greatness of his malice that, as the schoolmen determine, it cannot admit any farther degree of augmentation; his will is immovably fixed to evil as its ultimate end. Therefore his malice and hatred must dispose him to do such evils as may bear a proportion to the greatness of them. And wherein can it in a higher way reveal itself than in designing and effecting the ruin of the souls of men by pernicious counsels and devices? If there is any one thing in which so discontented a person as Satan is can take delight, it is in his trade of seduction and destruction in making others as irrecoverably lost and miserable as he himself is.

As tempting and ensnaring men is his only business, so his diligence in it is matchless. He was going to and fro in the earth, and walking up and down in it in Job's time (Job 1:7). In Peter's time he was a roaring lion, walking about, seeking whom he may devour (1 Peter 5:8). The beasts of the earth hunt their prey, yet when the sun rises and man goes forth to labor, they gather themselves together and lay down in their dens (Psalm 104:22). But this infernal lion is restless in his motions, and compasses the earth with as much unweariedness as the sun does the heavens. It is true, he tempts others to idleness, but he himself is never idle. The fowler is desirous that the flying bird would light upon the ground or perch upon some tree; and when it does so it better becomes his mark. So the devil does what he can to lull others asleep in idleness and sloth; but he then does not cease to shoot his darts and spread his snares.

When Samson was asleep on Delilah's knees, she caused his locks to be cut off (Judges 16:19), and wrought all that mischief upon him that did not terminate in the loss of his eyes, but in the loss of his life. While the servants slept the enemy came and sowed his tares (Matthew 13:25). Oh, how well would it go with Christians if the diligence of their adversary would provoke them to watchfulness, and kindle in them a holy industry unto all good, so that they might prove themselves to be God's soldiers to fight against all evil, and God's workmen and servants to do all good. Surely their complaints would be fewer and their comforts would be greater.

But, alas, what a sad complaint I now take up. And while I speak of the diligence of the evil one, I mourn over the security and negligence of most professing Christians, among whom a waking eye and a working hand are as rare to be found as a sword and a spear among all the people of Israel (1 Samuel 13:22)! How few are there who have taken the alarm, though they are called upon to stand watch against temptations? How hard it is to persuade men that to walk circumspectly is a duty, or that to be diligent in their callings is one of the best antidotes to perserve the soul from the putrefaction of lusts, and to fence it against the incursions of an assiduous tempter! It is a common proverb that the lion is not as fierce as he is painted; and it is a received opinion that the devil is not so hurtful an enemy as he is represented to be. It is no wonder then if his designs are so successful and his triumphs many, when the greatest part of men are in no way anxious to proportion their care and watchfulness to either the greatness of their own danger or their adversary's diligence.

DEMONSTRATION 4. A fourth demonstration which may discover the power of Satan to tempt is taken from both the number of the evil spirits and the unity of their counsels, which meet all in one common center of an irreconcilable hatred to God's glory and man's happiness.

First, their numbers are great, which renders their power as well as their counsels exceedingly dreadful. Weak things, which when few are contemptible, when seconded with multitude become irresistible. Caterpillars, frogs, locusts, and flies, by the excess of their number, made the proud heart of Pharaoh to stoop, who could not free himself or his kingdom from such impotent adversaries. The whale, of which God said that upon the earth there is not his equal ("he is a king over all the children of pride" Job 41:34), of all creatures in the sea or on the land that pride themselves in their might and strength, he is the chief. And yet Pliny said that the herrings, by their vast numbers, oppress and destroy sometimes the biggest whales. How dreadful then must that opposition be that arises from such creatures that are in their nature powerful, and for their numbers past finding out.

The schoolmen who would seem to be expert Benjamites, who hit at a hair's breadth every mark at which they aim and do not miss, speak as confidently of the number of good and evil angels as if they had looked into the muster roll of both the heavenly host and the infernal legions; and yet their assertions have as little agreement with each other as the testimonies of the false witnesses concerning Christ—no two of them speak the same thing. Aquinas conceived the number of them in their creation to exceed incomparably all material substances, and his reason, as Estius sets it down, is, because the more perfect any beings are in their nature, the greater is their excess, either of magnitude, if they are corporeal, or of number, if they be noncorporeal. As the heavenly bodies, which are most perfect, wonderfully surpass all inferior bodies in quantity, so do the spiritual angels in number.

Now of these vast numbers, say some, the one half became apostates. Others, from a mistaken interpretation of Revelation 12:4, where the dragon draws a third part of the stars of heaven after him, have fondly concluded that a third part of them fell, when it plainly speaks of a defection in the church. Others have made the number of fallen angels equal to the number of the elect who shall be saved, who are to supply the breach that was by their defection. But what light or evidence do any of these positions carry in them that may gain the understanding of sober men to a belief of them? Are they not niceities, that are as unfit to build upon as the dreams of sick men? It is enough that the Scripture, though it does not acquaint us with the certain number of good or evil angels, that of the one it tells us that there are thousand thousands that minister unto God, and ten thousand times ten thousand that stand before Him (Daniel 7:10). There is an innumerable company of angels (Hebrews 12:22). And Scripture represents to us the evil angels by a kingdom, which implies multitudes, and by a prince, whose greatness lies to the extent of his condition and the number of his subjects. Surely we need no hermit's visions to inform us that the air is full of malignant spirits, and the earth of their snares to entrap the inhabitants of it. Paul points out to us their number as well as their power when he says that we do not wrestle with flesh and blood, but against "principalities, against powers, against the rulers of the darkness of this world, against spiritual wickedness in high places" (Ephesians 6:12). Oh, what a troublesome passage must every Christian expect in his way to heaven, who is to conflict with armies of these infernal Anakims? How necessary is it that he put on the armor of God for protection, and fight in the strength of God to obtain a victory? For in his own might no man can prevail. If Elijah, a prophet of a

heroic spirit, complained of his being left alone to
contest with the priests of Baal and the idolaters of
Israel, so as to grow weary of his life, how apt will the
best of men be to faint and sink in the long and sharp
conflicts that must be undergone with the combined
forces and powers of darkness if not aided and
supported by the strength of Christ? If therefore we
would be successful combatants in this spiritual
warfare, we must do as David did, who prepared to
encounter Goliath by disarming himself of his warlike
habiliments, and going forth only in the name of the
Lord of Hosts. We must put off all carnal confidence,
which will be as useless to us as Saul's armor was to
David, and be strong only in the Lord, and in the power
of His might. This is what will both animate us in the
fight and give unto us an assured victory in the issue.

Second, as their number is great, so their unity and
agreement is wonderful. In Satan's kingdom there are
no divisions (Matthew 12:26). In his armies there are no
mutinies for lack of pay, no complaints of hard
marches, though they are continually compassing the
earth to and fro. That there should be a union among
the heavenly host is not strange, in regard they are all
as so many melodious instruments tuned to one key;
they are as so many needles touched with the same
magnet, which fixes them invariably to one point. They
dwell with and in Him who is love itself. But is it not a
matter of admiration that an entire oneness, which is
so much wanting on earth, should be found in hell?
What is hell but the common sewer and drain into
which those lusts of pride, wrath, envy, and bitterness,
from whence wars arise, empty themselves? Have devils
any love? Is there any print of that noble quality, which
is as amiable as the sun, to be found in the territories of
darkness? What then is that ligament or cement that so
firmly ties and joins them together? It is no other but a

perfect hatred for both God and man, it being the one thing designed by them to rob God of His glory and man of his happiness; and to effect this, the conspiracy is strong and the league inviolable. The good angels rejoice at the conversion of a sinner, and the evil angels at his destruction. Ruined sinners are the only trophies and spoils of hell.

Oh, blush then you saints, who have so many sacred bonds to unite you to God, and also to one another, and yet by divisions are set at a distance from each other, making the enemies valiant by your discords! Are you not all the brethren of one Father, God blessed forever? Are you not of one Mother, Jerusalem, which is above, brethren of the same blood, like Joseph and Benjamin? Have you not suckled the same breasts, and been nursed up with the same sincere milk of the Word? Are you not all joint heirs of the same glorious inheritance, reserved for you in the heavens? Are you not led by the same Spirit of God, who is a Spirit of love and goodness? He does not beget birds of prey, but doves, whose bills are never seen to be bloody in the least. Shall not then love effect that in you which a cursed hatred does in devils? They are one by a common principle of wickedness which runs through them; and shall not you be one who are so closely knit together with so many and such strong ties? That the lustful goats should push at one another is not a matter of wonder, but that the tender lambs should doss and strike at each other cannot bring anything but a lamentation.

DEMONSTRATION 5. A fifth demonstration of Satan's power and ability to tempt is from his great and strange ability to convey suggestions to evil after such a manner into the heart that they cannot be distinguished from the lustings and ebullitions of depraved nature. It is not only difficult to find out any certain

character between the evil that is sown and the evil that
is inbred, between the bitings of the serpent and the
disease of the mind, as Bernard expresses it, but it is
wholly impossible. He professed that after much search
and study he could never clearly know what he may
charge upon his heart and what upon the Tempter.
Now his advantage of thus insinuating and winding
himself into the bosom much promotes and furthers a
compliance with his suggestions, because men are
more apt to be swayed by such thoughts which they
look upon as the natural births of their own hearts
than ever they would be by such which they discern to
be foreign, and to be injected from an irreconcilable
and a sworn enemy. If any print or signature of Satan's
did in the least appear in his suggestions, by which the
tempted might discover when the motions to any sin
came from him and when from themselves, neither
success nor their danger would be so great by far as
now they both are. For it cannot be reasonably imagined that any should so readily close with or hearken
unto what they find him to be the prompter of, as to
what they deem to have its rise from their own breast,
without any other mover than themselves.

The bird takes the egg or young for its own, though
secretly put into the nest by another hand, which therefore, with an unwearied diligence, it both hatches and
feeds; but if it should once discover that it is not its
own, it forthwith casts it out and destroys it as spurious.
And so those sinful motions which are injected into
mens' hearts by the evil one, but are reputed by them to
be none other than the natural births of their own
minds, are more dandled in their thoughts, and sooner
gratified by an actual compliance, than ever they would
be if discovered to have their origin from the Tempter.
When Satan stood up against Israel and provoked David
to number the people (1 Chronicles 21:1), it was not by

making such impressions as might evidence him to be the counselor of the fact, but by exciting such affections of vainglory and self-confidence which naturally abound in the hearts of princes when their armies are victorious, and the face of their affairs like a serene sky without any mixture of clouds.

Benhadad grew in his demands upon Ahab, as if he would try what it was that he dared deny by adding a second message to his first one, in which he enlarged the terms of his submission to the searching of his house and the houses of his servants, and then taking away whatsoever was desirable in their eyes. Then, being refused the doing of it, he proudly boasted that the dust of Samaria shall not suffice for handfuls for all the people that followed him (1 Kings 20:10).

Sennacherib, fleshed with the many conquests that he had obtained over divers nations, swelled with pride till he broke out into blasphemy: "Who are they among all the gods that have delivered their country out of my hands, that the Lord should deliver Jerusalem out of my hands?" (2 Kings 18:35). Yea, good Hezekiah had his heart so far lifted up within him by the fulness of his treasures, and the multiplicity of his provisions for both war and peace, that he vainly boasted of them to the ambassadors of the king of Babylon (2 Chronicles 32:31).

And from such latent seeds of pride, which breed in the best of hearts as moths in the finest garments, Satan kindled this inordinate desire in David to know the number of his warlike forces, which the just expostulations of Joab and the captains of the Host could not allay. He delighted in this thing, and the king's word prevailed (2 Samuel 24:3–4).

In tempting Christ, Satan made use of Peter's natural affection for his Master to dissuade him from suffering death (Matthew 16:22). Little did Peter suspect that

the words which he spoke Satan prompted, and that he
was but an instrument to convey the poison of a temptation as black as hell into his Savior's bosom, the consequences of which would have been more dismal than
if the stars had dropped from heaven, the sun been
blotted out of its orbit, or the whole creation had become as shriveled parchment before the fire. For what
would have become of all the chosen of God? Must they
not have died *in* their sins if Christ had not died *for*
their sins? Must not heaven have been empty of glorious saints within, though thick set with glittering stars
without? Must not the work of redemption have been
like the structure of an unwise builder, who began to
build but never finished what he had begun? But, alas,
all these astonishing evils were not in the least discerned by Peter, much less designed. Little did he
think of being a tempter to his Lord, or of receiving
such a check from Christ as to have his name given to
him whose work he did: "Get thee behind Me, Satan."
And in this mysterious and hidden way he still man-
ages his suggestions in the hearts of both believers and
others also, so that their compliance might be more
facile to the evil to which he tempts, while he is not de-
tected to be the first mover to it. Old Isaac would not
have been persuaded to have eaten of Jacob's venison,
though he greatly loved it, if he could have discerned,
either by questioning who he was or by feeling his
hands, him not to be his son Esau.

So though men have a secret liking to the sin to
which they find themselves moved, yet if the instigations unto it appeared to them to come from Satan, it
would rather make them tremble, as Isaac did when
Jacob's subtlety was found out, than in any way beget in
them further hankerings to hasten to fulfill it. But that
which makes the mystery of his undiscerned impressions the more strange is that though in the same

temptation he reiterates the deception again and again, yet is it not more perceived by us at the last than it was at first. We are still at as great a loss to trace out any difference between his injections, and the natural lustings of the heart to evil as we would be to find the path of a serpent uon a rock: though it passes often over the rock, yet it does not leave, as worms and snails do, any filth or slime behind it that may display his various and crooked windings.

DEMONSTRATION 6. A sixth demonstration, with which I shall close this first general heading of Satan's ability to tempt, is from the suitableness that is between his suggestions and our corrupt reason. He cannot in the least offer violence to the soul, or break in upon it by a forcible entry whether it will or not. The body may be liable to his violence, but not the soul. The assertion of Bonaventure is true: "The devil may allure, God alone can effectually change, but none can compel us." When therefore he tempts to sin, he insinuates himself by such topics as are pleasing to carnal reason, and apt to beget a ready compliance with his suggestions. To profane and atheistic wretches, he suggests that religion is but a cunning and devised fable, a mere scarecrow, set up by preachers to keep simple and weak people in awe; that heaven and hell, things so much spoken of, are but imaginations—the one a pleasing dream, and the other a false fire, that frightens more than it hurts, and that they which seem to dread it most are yet sometimes venturous enough to do such things from which a flaming Tophet should wholly restrain them. Now what dry tinder sensual hearts are to such suggestions that fall upon them as sparks! Who can be so blind as not to perceive? Are not these their secret wishes, that there were no God to judge them, and no hell or prison of burning flames to torment them? Do they not do what they can to cut off the hand of con-

science that it may not smite them, and to put out its
eyes that it may not see them? How easily then are they
drawn into that opinion which they would gladly have
to be a truth? And how justly left of God are they to such
horrible delusions, that sinning without fear they may
perish without remedy?

Others again, who by convictions are awakened to
some more serious apprehensions of God and religion,
by specious suggestions he persuades that the strictness
of life which some few pretend unto is but an affecta-
tion of singularity, in which they strive not so much to
be like God as to be unlike their neighbors, that it is a
heavy yoke which they put upon themselves, and none
of that easy yoke and light burden which Christ com-
manded them to take upon themselves. They need not
fear but that they shall speed well enough, though they
are not so scrupulous as others, who stick at every small
matter as if salvation consisted altogether of punctilios,
and could never be obtained without an arrival at the
highest pitch of sanctity. If they pray sometimes when
they think of it, read the Scripture when their leisure
best serves them, and see the church now and then in
fair weather, it is as much as is needed.

Are not these whisperings of the serpent of an en-
chanting nature? Are not these kind of reasonings
suited to most mens' tempers, who in religion affect
rather to discover that invisible point where grace and
nature part than to pursue after attainment of a perfect
stature in holiness? Men think that a taste of godliness,
like a little medicine on the knive's point, is more desirable than making it a man's daily food. Men deem a
slight tincture of religion useful to themselves, and yet
nauseate as some abominable thing the deep and double dye of it, so as to have it like a prevailing principle
to give a law and rule to their whole conversation. The
ground becomes fruitful not by receiving, but by

accepting the seed that is cast into it. Just so, temptations become successful not by the heart's bare reception of them, but by its secret relishing and affecting of them.

If Satan, who is the evil seedman, scatters any seeds of temptations, to which the heart is as a prepared and disposed soil by the corrupt principles that lodge in it, they will quickly sprout forth into acts, and grow into a root that will bear gall and wormwood. Can I then better put a period to this first general heading than by giving the good Christian a brief yet serious caution to listen to those corrupt reasonings with which Satan often feathers those arrows of temptation that are shot out of his bow, that they may the better reach the mark to which they are directed? Man is a reasonable creature, and is apt to be swayed by anything that carries a semblance of reason. And if sin comes in any such dress, the will is soon gained to embrace the motion, and the sin itself to be finished, which the apostle tells us bringeth forth death (James 1:15).

Chapter 4

An Enumeration of Satan's Wiles

A great part of my designated task is to discover the policies and devices of this grand master of craft, not by compiling an entire body or system of them, or undertaking to give an exact and just account of their number, which is a work as hopeless as counting the stars and calling them by their names, but by singling and choosing out of the full heap some which in the spiritual warfare are of most frequent use, and are of greatest danger, so that so every soldier of Christ who is engaged in it may see what need they have to exercise watchfulness as well as courage, having to do with an adversary who is no less active in his subtleties than he is implacable in his malice. I would rather be cautious than valiant; the valiant are often ensnared, but the cautious seldom are.

DEVICE 1. It is a pernicious device and wily strategy of Satan's to tempt by method, and by the practice of lesser sins to make the way more facile for the commission of greater ones. He casts down none suddenly from the pinnacle of a high profession into the lowest abyss of wickedness, but leads them rather by oblique descents and turnings, lower and lower, until at last they take hold of hell. The beginnings of sin, as well as of grace, may fitly be resembled to a grain of mustard seed, which is of all seeds the least; but the growth of it is such that the birds of the air come and lodge in the branches thereof. Sin appears at first like Elijah's cloud, and afterwards darkens the whole face of heaven. It is as the head of a river, which has no breadth or depth, yet by its running increases and swells into the similitude of a sea.

Small offenses, by Satan's industry, become the parents of signal crimes. Has not anger, which sets no other bounds to itself than blood and death, taken its rise from a small disgust or dislike, as sometimes a deadly gangrene comes from a slight prick of an artery? Have not completed impurities often derived themselves from the glance of a wanton eye, or from some light and foolish gesture? Was the beginning of those complicated sins in David, his murder and adultery, not an unhallowed look? Did not lust, which like a moral jaundice spreads its deformity over the whole man, display itself at first in the eye?

It is Calvin's observation that those expressions in Psalm 1 of "walking in the counsel of the ungodly, of standing in the way of sinners, and sitting in the seat of the scornful," point out how by little and little men turn aside from the right way. First, they hearken to wicked counsels and solicitations to sin, which are as the seed of evil actions; then the devil entices them to join themselves in fellowship with sinners, till at length they become proud mockers, scorning both the reproofs of men and the judgments of God; finally, through depraved principles of conscience, they speak good of evil and evil of good. Now, how this gradual manner of Satan's tempting serves his design of drawing men to sins of the greatest scandal and presumption, we may easily see if we do but consider that lesser sins make way for greater ones in four ways:

• First, by way of deception. Men think of little sins as they do of slight distempers in the body: they are soon mastered and overcome. An ordinary decoction, a gentle sweat, or a few meals' abstinence are valid enough prescriptions to gain a clear riddance of a distemper; and a resolution or two taken up of leaving

what has been done, or of doing otherwise than before,
will as readily cure the small sins. But there is no custom so weak that does not have more power over our
nature than we intended first to give it, insomuch that
many have been overborne with those actions, the effects whereof they presume to be at their own disposal.
For as children turn round so long in sport till at last
they fall down when they would stand, so there are
many who indulge themselves in little slips and failings, and thereby bring themselves to such an evil
dizziness of mind as throws them down when they purpose to stand and to break off from the paths in which
they walked. When therefore a man finds that he is
tempted to sin because it is a little one, and may at any
time be as easily left as taken up, let him look upon it as
a double imposture of the devil, who if he makes it
seem little in or before the doing of it, can make it appear much greater when it is done. Or, if he would persuade him that it may without difficulty be left, let him
remember there is a wide difference between running
up a hill and running down a hill: he who runs up a
hill may stop when he will, but may not do so if he runs
down. So if a man is climbing the hill of grace, he may
sit down or slack his pace as he pleases; but once he
steps down the hill of a bad life, he can hardly give over
till he comes to the very bottom of it, till he has finished his sin, which, when it is finished, brings forth
death (James 1:15).

• Second, by way of disposition. Small sins are as the
priming of a post or pillar, that prepare it to better receive those other colors that are to be laid upon it, and
in which it is to stand; or as the previous dippings of
the wool in divers liquors that it may drink in more
fully the tincture of the scarlet. They beget powerful inclinations in the soul to greater sins, and make a way
for their entrance by corrupting men's apprehensions

of sin, both in respect of its deformity and its magnitude, no sin being equally ghastly and big to look on to him who admits familiarity with the least of sins, as to him who abstains from all appearance of evil. It is Josephus's observation that Solomon's foul defection to those stupendous impieties of idolatry, and the inordinate love of many strange women, got its beginning from some lesser slips and failings against the law of God, such as his setting the Brazen Sea upon twelve oxen, and making the figures of lions and cherubims upon its borders. And to him, and other ancient Hebrews who are of the same opinion, Grotius inclines, adding also his multiplying of chariots and horses against the express command of God in Deuteronomy 20:1 as another lapse before his strange departing and forsaking of the way. I shall not make it my work to determine what special warrant Solomon might have for what was done by him about things of the temple, which would free him from that part of the charge; but I think that whoever looks into his penitential book of the Preacher may easily find that his fall was not perpendicular, and such which at once cast him as low as ever any of the holy men of God fell, but a sinking and sliding downwards by degrees. Hence from him learn, who was the wisest man who ever was or shall be, that it is not wisdom that will keep a man from the worst of sins, if he once allows or favors himself in lesser evils.

• Third, by way of subtraction, and withholding that which may hinder the commission of greater sins. The powerful preservatives against presumptuous evils are an awful fear of God and a heart touched with the due sense of sin. "How can I do this great wickedness and sin against God," was Joseph's plea to his master's wife when she tempted him to folly (Genesis 39:9). David's heart, when tender, smote him for an irreverent touch of Saul's garment as well as for the cruel murder of

Uriah (1 Samuel 24:5). Now both of these preservatives
a customary living in small sins will waste and destroy
by making the heart brawny and stiff; a path that is fre-
quently trodden only by the foot of a child will contract
a hardness as well as the beaten road, and so will the
heart in which little sins have a common passage too
and fro, as well as the heart that is as the highway that
leads to destruction; for all sin has the same tendency,
though it does not work the effect in the like degree. As
they who would keep themselves from a confirmed
stone use daily helps to carry away the smaller gravel,
so, to prevent a flinty and obdurate heart, the care must
be constant, and the practice frequent, of purging the
conversation from little sins.

Once the exercise of this duty is neglected, it can
hardly be imagined how suddenly men come to do
worse than ever. How is it that men sport themselves in
the commission of those sins, at the mention of which
they would once have trembled, and brutishly wallow in
the midst of that mire, the least speck of which they
would not formerly have allowed to be found on their
garments? Is it not their compliance with lesser sins
that makes them disregard greater ones? Is it not from
their neglect of the fear of God, a powerful antidote
against the growth of sin? This is made the cause by
God Himself of Israel's multiplied wickedness in
Jeremiah 9:3: " 'They proceed from evil to evil, and they
know not Me,' saith the Lord."

• Fourth, by way of palliation, and hiding them
when done. All sin, as it has death for its wages
(Romans 6:23), so it has shame for its companion;
thence it is that men seek to cover one sin with another, deeming it better to be guilty of two faults than
to be convicted of one. And usually a greater sin is
made the covering of a lesser one, as the vizard which is
worn to disguise and hide a person's deformity is more

deformed than the face that it covers. At the angel's tidings that she should have a child, Sarah laughed; and when he observed it she denied it (Genesis 18:15). To hide one sin she committed another; she told a lie to free herself from the charge of laughter. And this second sin, if circumstances be weighed, will be found greater then the first.

David, to conceal his adultery with Bathsheba, covered it with the murder of Uriah her husband—a strange figleaf to spread over so foul a crime, but where will not the shame of sin drive a man if so holy a person as David could be secure in having done evil to do worse. That excellent woman Eudocia the Empress, wife of Theodosius the younger, had an apple given to her by the Emperor that was wonderfully large, that had been presented to him as a rarity. She bestowed it upon Paulinus, a learned person; he, not knowing from whom the Empress had received it, offered it to the Emperor. The Emperor sent for his wife and asked her for the apple. She, fearing that her giving it away might displease the Emperor, answered that she had eaten it. He urged her to tell the truth, but she swore that she had eaten it. Upon this the incensed Emperor brought forth the apple as a testimony against her, and in his jealousy killed innocent Paulinus, and hated his own wife, who before was greatly beloved by him. Is it not then a matter of complaint as well as of wonder that this practice should be the common salve that many use to make others deem them innocent when they have done evil, to add to denials oaths, curses, and bitter imprecations of themselves, little regarding what guilt they contract before God so long as they may seem blameless before men. But let such know that they sow the wind and shall reap the whirlwind, and that as they cover one work of darkness with another, God shall add one judgment to another, and by the scorching flames of His wrath shall make them to read the truth of that divine maxim: "He that hideth his sins shall not prosper, but whoso confesseth and forsaketh them shall have mercy" (Proverbs 28:13).

DEVICE 2. A second device and circumvention of Satan is a vexatious and restless importunity in urging to doing that sin to which he tempts. In this temptation there are three parts:

First, suggesting or casting evil thoughts into the mind. In John 13:2 it is said that the devil put it into the heart of Judas to betray his Master. He threw, as a dart, that thought into him, finding it then a fit season both for him to make such a motion and for Judas to receive it.

Second, persuading, or backing the suggestion with arguments which may sway the understanding to approve and incline the will to consent to that evil as good. He presses sometime by way of terror, propounding sad events that will undoubtedly follow if there is not a yielding to what is suggested. Thus many are moved to a practice of stealing and deceiving through a conceived fear of want and poverty which will else inevitably fall on them. Others are moved to lying and perjury to preserve their life and liberty, which may be otherwise hazarded if not lost. Thus Peter both denied and forswore his Lord to save himself from that danger which his being with Him might otherwise have exposed him to.

Sometimes Satan does this by way of enticement, setting before them the profit and advantage that will accrue by their compliance with his motion. Thus Ahab's prophets, through the suggestion of a lying spirit, persuaded him to go up to Ramoth-Gilead because of the prosperous success that would attend his undertaking (1 Kings 22:21). And with a far more alluring bait would the devil have courted our Savior to have done homage and obeisance unto him by promising to invest Him with a right to all the kingdoms of the world upon that single condition (Matthew 4:9).

Third, a vehement and continued instigation to speedily execute what is suggested. This is the utmost extent of satanic power. 1 Chronicles 21:1 says that Satan stood up against Israel and provoked David to number the people. The Syriac version renders it, "He hurried David headlong," not by compelling him, but with instance again and again enforcing the motion till it was effected, notwithstanding Joab's just expostulations and averseness to it. The rule of fencing is (said Lypsius) *repete* double, and follow the blow when made. That is also Satan's practice, who pursues oftentimes his suggestions with that violence so as to rob men of their sleep so that they may wake to his temptations; to urge them, whether in company or alone, whether in their callings, and recreations or in their solemn duties to God, to give them no freedom nor respite till he gains that from them by importunity which he could not by argument and persuasion.

Now how powerful a means this is to obtain an end when persisted in, and after received denials and repulses to turn opposition into yielding, the Scripture will furnish us with full and pregnant evidence. What was it that drew from Samson the discovery of that secret that cost him his life but Delilah's restless importunity? She pressed him daily with her words, and urged him so that his soul was vexed unto death (Judges 16:16). He whom the combined power of the Philistines could not overcome was foiled by the flattering solicitations of a woman, so as to become both their laughter and their prey. What was it that made the unjust judge in the parable to resolve to avenging the widow of her enemies but a fear lest, by her continual coming, she should weary him (Luke 18:5). The original word is very emphatic, which Beza renders, "Lest she should beat or buffet him." It is the same as in 1 Corinthians 9:27: "I keep under my body, and bring it into subjection," alluding to the Roman *Cestus,* in which kind of fight it was the aim of the adversary to bring the other to stoop and fall under his blows. Yea, our Savior seems to ascribe a more prevailing power to importunity than to friendship, that the one will extort what the other cannot entreat. Luke 11:8: "I say unto you, though he will not rise and give him because he is his friend, yet because of his importunity he will rise and give him."

Can it then be a matter of wonder to any Christian, as if some strange thing had befallen him, to find himself not only tempted to evil, but incessantly pressed with vehemence to do it? Or need he, as not knowing the cause of his trouble, inquire as Rebekah did, "Why am I thus?" Is not Satan a subtle enemy? And is it not his designed aim to make the life of every believer either uncomfortable or unholy, the one by an irksome importunity to evil, the other by a consent and yielding to doing it? Is it not one of his arts and methods to work a despondence in those who resist him, by continuing his assaults after a long and tedious conflict in which they have born up against him, so that, despairing of being conquerors, they may yield themselves as captives? Yea, has he not by this policy staggered many Christians, so as to make them say those evil words (as Parisiensis calls them), "I am overcome," and so to choose rather to sin than any longer to endure the trouble of his assaults? It is true, perhaps, that such who have not experienced the continued violence of Satan's instigations in this kind, of putting them upon the commission of a particular sin, may judge it no hard task to persist in the denial of it, and to turn a deaf ear to all his solicitations and importunity, it being easy to conceive many things to be more facile than we find them to be when assayed. But to them who think thus, I recommend you duly weigh these three considerations:

• The frailty and weakness of the flesh, which can as ill bear long temptations as long afflictions. What the length of afflictions will expose unto, David hints to us when he says, "The rod of the wicked shall not rest upon the lot of the righteous, lest the righteous put forth their hands unto iniquity" (Psalm 125:3). And will not the rod of the wicked one do as much by its long continuance? The devil knows, said Luther, that we are earthen vessels which cannot always bear multiplied knocks and violent strokes; and therefore those whom he cannot bend to his will by force and fraud, he seeks to overcome by a continued importunity, and in this way he vanquishes many, who lack the patience to endure, though they have at first the courage to resist.

• The art that Satan mingles with his violence. His urgency is not to a course and way of sin, but to the single act and commission of it. That which is often repeated and said over by him in his pressing of it is, "Do it just once; try it just this time. Why not once? Why not now? Is it not better to ease ourselves of the vexation by yielding once to the motion than to be always under it?" He knows that if a sin is once committed it will leave a proneness to do it again; and if the terrors of doing it, which are commonly greatest at first, are once broken through, it will not be a matter of difficulty to obtain the consent to doing it the second and third time because the heart must be less bent against it in prayer, and the power of grace and faith less vigorous to resist it when weakened by yielding to sin, conscience also less tender and affected with the sense of it.

• The inequality of temper which is in the best. Grace, that makes the opposition to temptations that are both violent and long, does not always work alike in the soul, any more than the pulse beats alike in the body. Grace sometimes has operations that are quick and strong, and at other times such as are slow and languid. There are none who stand quite out of the shadow of sin, though out of the region of death. Can it therefore be an easy work to bear up against Satan's pressing instigations unto evil, when the spiritual part is often clogged and made less active by the flesh, yea, when it is weakened by its treachery? Surely, were it not that the mercies of Christ were moved in Him unto His own when they are in such a condition, as He was towards Peter when Satan desired to sift him as wheat, their faith would fail. Let me then speak compassion to all those who labor under the relentless importunities of the Tempter who for days, months, and years prompts them to some one sin, and they are no more able to flee from these temptations than to outrun themselves; no more able to cast them off than to shake off their own flesh.

To any who have tasted the sweetness of holiness, what can be more hateful than daily instigations to sin? And to such who understand the blessedness of communion with God, what can be more bitter than to find themselves chained fast, as it were, to a devil, who continually makes such applications of vile objects to their fancy that they cannot turn in the least from? If it were burdensome to Antipheron Orietes, whom Aristotle reported to always behold his own image standing before him, how irksome must it be to a gracious heart to be always haunted with the spectacle and image of some sin as black as hell? May I not say then on their behalf what Hezekiah spoke by his messengers to Isaiah in 2 Kings 19:3–4: "This day is a day of trouble, and of rebuke, and blasphemy. . .wherefore lift up a prayer for them." Oh, pray that God would be their shield, and His power might be manifested in their weakness, so that the evil one might not touch them with any assimilating touch. Pray that, though he molests them, yet he may not defile them; that though he fights against them, yet he may not prevail over them; but that with the temptation God would make a way to escape so that they may be able to bear it.

DEVICE 3. A third device and policy of the prince of darkness is ceasing to tempt, or after some short conflict to feign a flight, not from necessity but from design. It is said in Joshua 8:15 that Joshua and all Israel made as if they were beaten before the men of Ai, and fled by the way of the wilderness. But it was to draw them from their fenced city into an ambush they had set to ensnare them. Among other strategies which Brasidas in Thucidides calls the thefts of war, Satan often uses this one: pretending a flight that thereby he may better steal a victory and bring unlooked-for mischief upon those from whom he seems to fly. Parisiensis says that this one is of all his snares and wiles the most dangerous, because as he designs it for evil ends, so it seldom fails to succeed.

Few observe whether his flight is pretended or real, whether his ceasing to tempt is out of skill, in order to some hidden design, or out of constraint caused by the resistance of faith. I shall therefore endeavor to show what Satan aims at in his seeming flight, how to distinguish it from that which is real and forced by the firm opposition which faith makes against him, and the victory faith obtains over him.

First, by this policy he seeks to infect and swell the heart with pride, which to keep down and destroy is one great end of God's allowing His people to be tempted. Pride is a sin which it is hard to kill or to starve, so suitable a soil is the heart to nourish it above all other sins whatsoever, and so apt is every occasion to make it put forth afresh. But nothing more quickens and actuates it than greater achievements. It is Tacitus's observation, "Renowned generals are puffed

up with success, especially against an enemy of repute
and eminence." And is there any adversary who can
contribute more to his glory who puts him to flight
than the great Dragon, that old serpent called the devil
and Satan? Is not he the prince of the air, and the god
of this world? Are not his territories full of captives,
whom he has miserably enthralled? Has he not more
vassals than Christ has subjects? Must it not then be a
matter of just glory and triumph to defeat and overcome him, by whom such multitudes are vanquished?

But as he who strives must strive lawfully, so he who
glories must glory lawfully, which must be in the Lord,
in the power of whose might he is made strong—else
his glorying will be both his sin and snare. And this
Satan so fully understands that in the heat of a temptation he makes certain cessations and unexpected re-
tirements on purpose to deceive by the vain hopes of a
supposed victory. And are not many by this deceit lifted
up, as if their conflict were at an end and the field
wholly won by them? Do they not pride and please
themselves in thinking how they shook off that infernal viper with as much ease, and as little hurt to themselves, as Paul did the viper that came from the bundle
of sticks and fastened on his hand? Do they not slight
others who complain of long and sore temptations
with which they are buffeted, as if they sprang rather
from the weakness of the Tempter than the power? Oh,
when men thus set imaginary crowns on their own
heads, how unlike are they to those holy elders who
cast their crowns before the throne of God, saying,
"Thou art worthy, O Lord, to receive glory, and honor,
and power." And how like unto him whom they think
they have foiled by being tainted with that sin of pride,
which cast the angels out of heaven, and condemned
them to be reserved in everlasting chains under darkness unto the judgment of the Great Day.

Second, by this art he seeks to induce a spirit of security, and to possess the heart with vain presumption of a future peace and freedom from his assaults, than which nothing can prove more fatal to a spiritual warfare. That saying of Epicharmus, "Remember to distrust," is more useful counsel to none than to a Christian when not frowned upon by the world nor molested by Satan; for changes will come both from the one and the other. The world will prove to be a false friend, the devil a true Tempter. After three sharp repulses given him by our Savior, he departed only for a season (Luke 4:13). And can we expect that he will be beaten out of heart and made a coward by us? When resisted, and put to flight again and again, he will return, if not to conquer yet to vex. But nothing will more hasten his return than a drowsy security. That is the season which he watches for; that is the end of his ceasing to tempt and his seeming departure. And when he finds us, like the men of Laish, living careless and at ease (Judges 18:7), then he smites, not as the good angel did Peter, to awaken him (Acts 12:7), but to kill and destroy as much as in him lies. Then it is that he sows those noxious tares that come up afterwards to the prejudice and hurt of the good seed (Matthew 13:25). Then it is that he comes and brings seven worse spirits with him, making the last state of that man more miserable than the first (Luke 11:26). Let none therefore please themselves in a sinful ease and rest from temptations, as if the work were wholly done, when in truth nothing is done; but let them look how they come by it, and examine whether it is not a practice of the enemy rather than a reality; whether it does not rather spring from a ceasing of the Tempter to stir than from a victory obtained against him.

How to tell the difference between the one and the other is the next particular that I am to descend unto.

To find out therefore the truth of the one from the imposture of the other, I will set down briefly these three rules:

Look what means and ways of resistance have been used to put Satan to flight. Have instant prayers been made to God? Have the goings out against him been in the power and might of Christ? Has the Sword of the Spirit, which is the Word of God, been set against the motions of sin and the pressing instigations of the Tempter? What is it that has at any time been done to put a period to the conflict? As Livy said, "It is a folly to believe that by sitting still, and naked wishes, enemies can be conquered and overthrown." Victory attends the diligent and industrious, not the slothful. If then temptations vanish and disappear we know not how, and no account can be given of the calm and peace that we enjoy, as the fruits of prayer and other means used for obtaining it, we have cause to be jealous that the freedom and rest we have is but an artifice of the adversary to make us secure, and thereby the more easily to ensnare us. None are sooner vanquished than he who fears nothing.

Whenever Satan is really bested, sin is wounded. He is never put to flight but lust receives a mortifying blow; for the fight is both made and maintained by faith, and other graces of the Spirit, which carry in them a more immediate opposition unto sin than unto Satan. It is the great work of everyone who is begotten of God to keep himself, so that "the wicked one touch him not" (1 John 5:18). Not that he does not tempt him, but that he does not defile him by any assimilating touch. And this is the only way by which a believer can be said to both resist him and overcome him. We cannot kill the devil, nor in the least weaken his power; but as we mortify lusts, which are the matter that he works upon, and the less of it he finds in us, the less able he is to hurt us.

If therefore a temptation goes off, and the heart is not set more against sin so as to loathe and hate it, which is interpretative murder of sin as well as of our brother (1 John 3:15), so as to pray and watch more against it, we cannot well conclude our rest and ease to be good when it wants grace as its companion, and the quiet fruits of righteousness as its evidence (Hebrews 12:11).

When the wicked one is overcome and driven to flight, there will abide upon the soul a lively sense of so great a mercy. This will then manifest itself in a deep apprehension of those treacheries and deceits that the heart abounded with in the hour of trial, and a self-abhorrence for them in a humble and thankful acknowledgment of strength and power from Christ, whereby it is unable to fight a good fight, and to obtain a happy victory. The heart will carefully treasure up the experience it has had of God's faithfulness in its greatest straits, in a timely preparation and laying in of spiritual provisions for another encounter, knowing that its warfare will not be completed till it comes to heaven. These, and such like effects, are the issues of those temptations in which Satan is put to flight, and the ground of it is because it is done in the exercise of those means and graces of the Spirit as always leaves the soul in a better temper than it found it.

DEVICE 4. A fourth device of this spiritual Abaddon wherein he cheats thousands is by dividing the end from the means, or by busying them in the use of false and ineffectual means to attain the end, or by causing them to use good means in an undue and sinful manner.

It is a piece of Satan's sophistry to separate the means and the end, and to make men presume that though the one is neglected the other may be obtained; to this folly he would have tempted our Savior (Matthew 4:6). When he set Christ upon the pinnacle of the tem-

ple, he tempted Him to cast Himself down, and thereby
give proof of His sonship and God's fatherly care in
protecting Him. But as it is a sin to distrust God in the
want of means, it is no lesser sin to presume to be saved
without them when they may be had. It is not honoring
God by an absolute trust in Him, but tempting Him by a
wanton pride, in subjecting His power to act and work
according to our pleasure.

But though Christ has armed men against this
sophism of the Tempter by His own example, who
would not resort to reliance on God for safety in an extraordinary way when not debarred of the common and
usual way, how great is the number of those who tempt
God by unwarrantable practices, throwing themselves
into needless dangers and extremities so that His
power may appear in their deliverance and preservation? Cassian tells a story of three persons who, confident in God's providing for them, took a tedious jour-
ney into the desert, in which two of them miserably
died with hunger. Only the third returned as a sad
spectacle of their folly. Brentius relates the story of an
Anabaptist woman who invited many friends to supper,
but took no care to have anything to set before them,
presuming that the table would be furnished by God.
But what are these presumptions, in which men thus
divide between the end and the means, any other than
the scorn and laughter of those who deride their folly,
and yet, through the seduction of the devil, become
guilty of far greater ones? When they are confident of
heaven and careless of holiness, they are secure of the
end and yet tread not one step in the way that would
bring them to it. Are not these as vain as those who expect a harvest without a seedtime? Can any perish with
more clear self-convictions of God's justice in condemning them than these? Do they need to look into
the decrees of God to see the roots of their miscarriage,

or into their own consciences? May not they say that the serpent has beguiled them, while they have hearkened to the counsels of him who was a liar and a murderer from the beginning?

The subtlety of Satan touching the end and the means is seen in his putting men on the pursuit of those ways and mediums which do not in the least serve or conduce to the end for which they are used. So that, though the intended end is good, yet they fall as equally short of it as those who do nothing at all to obtain it, and are like misguided patients who by their medicines are not cured but killed. And who can count the thousands, or rather myriads, who are held under the power of this delusion of the devil? May we not ask the most of those who busy themselves in seeking a state of happiness, "Why do you lay out your money for that which is not bread? Why are you as those who build in the fire, where the structure consumes as fast as it is raised?"

Let us look abroad a little, and see if this is not true. Do we need to take a view of that strange and sudden spread of Mohammedanism? The seductions of this brutish impostor have prevailed to delude nations and kingdoms, who have subjected themselves to his laws and are drunk with the expectation of his carnal promises.

Or shall we confine our prospect to the Roman profession of religion? Though they impropriate salvation to themselves, and exclude all others who do not come within the pale and verge of their church, they have yet dangerously swerved from the rule and path of life. Harlot-like, they have laid the dead child in the room of the living child, their own corrupt fancies and inventions in the place of God's institutions, and in the observation of lying vanities forsake their own mercies. God has set in the Church—not as a trimmed lamp in

the sanctuary, but as the fixed sun in the firmament—
the good Word of His truth to disclose fully the knowledge of His will, which is the just measure of all that
obedience which He both requires and rewards. But in
this great luminary they have found what some as-
tronomers have of late discovered in the sun, a face
stained with dark spots; and therefore they charge it
with obscurity and defectiveness, taking unwritten tra-
ditions to be the guide and rule of their faith as well as
the Word—though all the light in them is but as the
blaze of a candle that is neither sweet nor certain.

God has called Himself a God who hears prayer, and
that unto Him all flesh shall come (Psalm 65:2). But
they have imparted this divine honor to saints, for
which they have neither precept, promise, nor example
in the Scriptures, robbing God of the glory of His
goodness, whose arms are always stretched out to receive those who come to Him in Christ's name. His
compassions are ever yearning towards their necessities, and ready to answer their prayers with his bounty.
So what need can there be of heavenly courtiers to render him more propitious to the fulfilling of their re-
quests? God has made eternal life to be of grace, not of
works, that it might be surely his gift (Ephesians 2:8–9).
It is His promise to them who love Him (James 1:12).
He has (as Augustine said) made Himself a Debtor not
by receiving anything from us, but by promising all to
us. But the Romanists, going about to establish their
own righteousness, have chosen rather to plead their
title unto it by way of right and justice, and to assert a
dignity and value in their works to which the reward is
due not of grace, but of debt. Can we think these are apt
mediums to bring the soul and salvation together? Are
they not rather chains of glass that are more specious
than strong? Are they not artifices rather then realities,
brought in by those who, in the apostle's dialect are se-

ducing spirits (1 Timothy 4:1), and are embraced by those who "received not the love of the truth that they might be saved" (2 Thessalonians 2:10)? Have we not then just ground to depart from the tents of these men, as Israel did from the tabernacle of Korah, Dathan and Abiram, and to touch nothing of theirs, lest we be consumed in all their sins? They may return unto us, but we cannot return unto them, according to God's command to the prophet (Jeremiah 16:19), unless we should change the truth of God into a lie, and serve the creature more than the Creator, who is blessed forever.

The subtlety of Satan touching the end and the means is seen also in making men miscarry in the use of right means by their using them in an undue manner, and so to fail of the end for which they are appointed by God. This is the way he prevails over multitudes of professing Christians whose duties, though done, daily prove wholly fruitless in the issue because of their heedless manner of performing them. Prayer is the key of blessing, which alone opens the treasures of heaven, both in regard of grace and comfort. And yet how many ask and do not receive because they ask amiss? The echo does not return an answer to every sound any more than God does every prayer. Duties without life provoke God rather than please Him, and gratify Satan rather than trouble him.

Satan does not care how much men hear, or how often they pray, if he can but allay their intention and fervency in both, by either distracting their minds or deadening their affections, so as to make them the skeletons of duties without a soul to enliven and actuate them, naked forms without any power of godliness. How contemptibly God speaks of His own institutions when done in a careless and loose manner! When Israel came to appear before Him, He asked who had required this at their hands, to tread His courts (Isaiah

1:12). Incense is an abomination, new moons and sab-
baths He cannot tolerate (verse 13). He cursed them as
deceivers who have in their flock a male, and then sacrifice unto the Lord a corrupt thing (Malachi 1:14).
And He threatened to spread the dung of their solemn
feasts upon their faces (Malachi 2:3).

Is it not then a matter of wonder as well as of complaint that those who own the appointed ordinances of
God to be the sole rule of giving glory to Him, and obtaining good from Him, should yet for the most part
satisfy themselves in doing duties rather than in the
fruits they reap from them? Is it not an interpretative
omission, though not a formal neglect, to make that to
be the task of the outward man which should be the
employment of the whole man; to be the work of the lip
that which should be the service of the heart? Will a
prayer that is like an arrow from a slack bow, which
never pierced the breast, ever pierce the heavens? Will
hearing the Word, when the running sands in the
hourglass are more eyed than the minister, ever convey
its sweetness to such an hearer? Will a sabbath that is
spent only in the forbearance of bodily labor, without
any ascensions of the soul to God in holy meditation,
or breathings after Him in fervent prayer, either fill a
man with the foretastes of heaven or make the fruition
of God in an eternal sabbath to be deemed as his only
happiness? And yet such schemes, such bodily exercises
which profit nothing, are the services which most give
unto God, presuming also that He is as well pleased
with them as themselves, while through the devil's craft
and the deceitfulness of their own hearts they look
upon them as evidences to difference them from both
the profane, who reject the thing that is good, and
from the erroneous, who are led out of the right way by
the fancies and inventions of men.

DEVICE 5. A fifth device and policy of Satan is his

strange and artificial dignifying of objects, so as to make them appear to be what they are not, yea, contrary to what they are in truth and reality. When Tamar designed to accompany Judah, her father-in-law, she put her widow's garments off, attired herself as a harlot, and sat in an open place (Genesis 38:14) so that she may better effect her purpose, and what the issue was the story tells us. So oftentimes, when Satan would allure and tempt to sin, he presents the object not in its natural dress, but clothed in such a manner as best suits what he aims at, and as may be easily seen in his attractives unto evil and his dissuasives from good.

First, evils which have a deformity inseparably cleaving to them he hides and palliates by giving them a superficial dye and tincture of virtue, whereby he many times deceives the uncautious, and serves also the hypocrite with specious pretenses. How the covetous person, whom the Lord abhors (Psalm 10:3), pleases himself in his sordid parcimony, as if he only practiced frugality, and followed the counsel of our Savior of gathering up the fragments so that nothing be lost (John 6:12)! With what a show of religion he denies bread to the hungry and clothing to the naked, while he shelters himself under the assertion of Paul that if anyone does not provide for his own house he has denied the faith and is worse than an infidel (1 Timothy 5:8). Yet his hand is shrunk up towards the one as well as to the other. He turns away from the stranger under a pretended care of providing for his family, and he robs them of their due necessities by making thrift a cloke for his avarice.

Is not also the Laodicean, or lukewarm professor, under the same delusion, in regard of the apprehensions he has of his spiritual state? Who prides himself more in his moderation and discretion than this one, as if he alone had hit the golden mean, and joined the wisdom of the serpent and the innocence of the dove together, being not overheated through the fiery passion of zeal, nor frozen and stupid through the dissoluteness of atheism and profaneness? Yet may not we say that that which is highly esteemed among men is an abomination in the sight of God? Has He not expressed how irksome such a temper is to Him, when for this very cause He threatens to spew a whole church out of His mouth (Revelation 3:16)? Yea, He seems to wish it rather to be wholly cold than to have such an imperfect participation in both the extremes—not but that cold is more remote from heat than lukewarmness; but yet as it is a state or condition it is worse, because men are very rarely, and with great difficulty, recovered out of it. Such are like those who lie in pleasant dreams and are loathe to be awakened out of them. It is Cassian's observation, which the experience of others may seal unto us as a truth: "Oftentimes of cold one is made hot; and of hot sometimes one returns to be cold; but seldom or never do any from lukewarm come to be hot."

So Satan allures to evil by covering its deformity with his artificial paint and varnish, so as to entitle it to the name of a virtue rather than of vice or sin. In so doing he is much like a deceitful coiner who stamps the king's image on his spurious metal to make it pass unsuspected.

Second, on the other hand, when Satan would dissuade from good, he represents it under the most contemptible form and appearance, to create such prejudices and dislikes against it as may cause them to apprehend that it is naturally of that complexion in which it appears to them. His intent is that by this means men may scorn the profession of it rather than embrace the practice of it, and look upon it as a thing that detracts from their worth and esteem, rather than adds anything to it. No broken glass can render a beautiful face more distorted and misshapen, either by multiplying the parts or misplacing them, than Satan does the most amiable things of grace and holiness.

Is it not through Satan's subtlety that religion itself has such an unpleasant aspect in most men's eyes? Is it not through the mists that he raises that it seems to be a dark and opaque body, and not a bright and glorious luminary, which fills the breast in which it is seated with light and peace? It is he who suggests to the atheist that to disdain it is a piece of reason, and to the profane that to neglect the profession of it, though they own the principles of it, is a point of gentility. It is he who makes the world judge the zealous Christian to be a fanatic, and the patient man who bears injuries without revenge to be a coward and stupid person who does resent affronts. It is Satan who makes the world judge him who exercises self-denial to his unruly appetites, and curbs with a strong rein the desires of the flesh, to be no better then a stoic fool, who seeks to reduce men to the condition of stocks and stones, and to eradicate all affections as abnormalities of nature rather than to cherish them as its genuine offspring.

Oh, how powerful are the arts and fascinations of this infernal magician, who can thus make men best pleased with that state in which they are rebels to God and slaves to lusts, and from which they can expect nothing but amazements, horrors, and distractions of mind, which will at one time or another afflict those who prostitute their consciences to such impieties as have in them the highest mixture of both folly and madness? Have we not need to remind men of Christ's counsel, "Judge not according to the appearance, but judge with righteous judgment" (John 7:24), when so many easily fall in love with gilded abominations, and greatly disesteem and scorn what is truly noble and di-

vine by the uncouth vizards that are put upon it? Have
we no need to set before men's eyes that woe that is de-
nounced against them who call evil good and good
evil, who put darkness for light and light for darkness
(Isaiah 5:20), when not a few are under the power of
strong delusions, and believe a lie? Surely it is not un-
necessary in this age of prodigious looseness, wherein
this imposture of Satan has so far prevailed that it is
thought pleasant enough to defend the worst of de-
baucheries, and to vindicate them from censure by the
putting upon them some light-hearted name—which is
the same as if a leper should expect to be reputed clean
because he has covered his foul ulcers with costly clothing, or as if a patient should be in love with his disease
because the physician calls it by some name which he
has purposely invented to please that patient's fancy.

DEVICE 6. A sixth device or machination (which
like the net cast on the right side takes multitudes, or
like the bow of Jonathan and the sword of Saul never
returns empty) is Satan's ensnaring all sorts of persons
in the use of lawful things. The adage is not more
common than true that we are undone by lawful things
rather than by sins. The smooth and deceitful stream
carries more to the whirlpool, which irrecoverably
sucks them in, than the rough and loud waters, which
frighten passengers from venturing upon them. Oh,
this is a great snare. Many men can give no account of
time, parts, or estates, but they can of hunting, drink-
ing, hawking, and so on. By his art and cunning, Satan
makes men transgress proper bounds in the use of
pleasures, recreations, nay, even necessary things.
Therefore take heed what you do, or how you walk, and
be sure to set boundaries to yourselves, remembering
that excess may turn that which is good into an absolute evil. Eating may become gluttony; industry in a
man's calling may become covetousness; recreations

may become looseness, when they are unbounded and not according to the rule and warrant of the Word.

DEVICE 7. The seventh wile of Satan is to suit his temptations to the ages and conditions of men.

Satan observes young years, middle age, and old age. He also observes the ages in Christianity, as the Apostle John shows in 1 John 2:12–13, where he writes to babes, young men, and fathers, as those who are subject unto various temptations and so need be cautious.

1. Young men he tempts to lust and wantonness; therefore Paul bids Timothy to flee youthful lusts (2 Timothy 2:22). And, oh, that I might prevail with young men to possess their vessels in holiness, and to remember their nature is that nature Christ has taken on Himself. It is the apostle's argument in 1 Corinthians 6:19 that your bodies are the temples of the Holy Ghost.

2. Satan tempts middle aged persons in that he stirs up an itch for honor and to be great, of building their families, and laying foundations of a name. And in this very snare many are caught who, by this very temptation, have their thoughts and minds so possessed that they willfully resist light, and put themselves upon courses that turn away their hearts from God. It is the thought and intent of many a man that, after he has feathered his nest and done so and so, he will think about his soul. Thus many of the popes sought the popedom by unlawful arts, especially Sylvester the Second.

3. Satan has temptations for old age, such as covetousness and peevishness.

Satan also observes the condition of men as well as their ages, and constitutions, the estates in which men are set. If men are afflicted and sad in spirit, he frightens them with fears and fancies that are as ghastly as the evils themselves. A melancholy person, whose fancy is like a broken glass, he fills with jealousies, surmises,

that make it swell as the water of jealousy did the belly
of the guilty woman. Oh, a dark heart is Satan's shop to
hammer his temptations in. If a man is poor, then
Satan tempts him to turn stones into bread, as he did
Christ when He was hungry; if rich, then to turn bread
into stones is the devil's alchemy. Thus he works with
men's states, conditions, humors, and passions, as
Agrippina did: when she poisoned her husband,
Claudius, she mingled the poison with the meat which
he loved most.

DEVICE 8. The eighth device is the insinuation of
many suggestions and temptations in such an indis-
cernable manner and way that we cannot discern or
differentiate them from the reasonings and thoughts
of our hearts; if men could so distinguish them, they
would not so easily hearken unto them. Bernard, in his
32 Sermons on Canticles [Song of Solomon] said, "It is
scarcely possible for any man to put an exact difference
between the biting of the serpent and the concupiscence and depravity of his own mind. I have not been
able to make any distinction between the things the
heart gives birth to and the evil tares the enemy sows
and casts in; it is most uncertain what I should attribute
to my self and what to him."

Now if Satan can thus cast in suggestions in such an
insensible manner, he must gain an advantage, because this way the gates of the soul are more readily
opened to him. If men apprehended that such and
such suggestions came immediately from the devil,
they would abhor to yield or hearken to them. But
when they apprehend them to be nothing but motions
and desires arising in themselves, they are more apt to
entertain them and comply with them. If Peter, when
he tempted Christ to spare Himself (Matthew 16:22),
had conceived the thought to have been from the devil,
certainly he would never have said it; but he looked

upon it only as the stirring of his own affections. If David had thought that the provocation to number the people had sprung from Satan, he would not have been so earnest in it. But that which makes this wile of Satan more dangerous is that, though he many times has circumvented us in this way, yet we do not know how to beware of him. If someone, through show of friendship or through flattery, has been injurious to us, we can ever after beware of him and not admit him to counsel us—but here it is otherwise. When Satan has today deceived us in this way, he may come again tomorrow and do it again, because we cannot discern his suggestions from our own thoughts.

Yet we may suspect them when we find that they are, first, against nature, such where the very shadow of a thought peeping out strikes the flesh into a trembling; second, when they are sudden and violent, like lightning; and third, when they are without reasonings, being accompanied with importunity. But the best remedy against this wile is not to be curious to distinguish between his suggestions and our concupiscence, but to be careful not to consent, and to remember that evil thoughts are the head of that old serpent.

DEVICE 9. The ninth wile, which is a very great subtlety and device of Satan, is in his delusions about doctrine, in seducing and drawing men aside into error by plausible opinions and doctrines that seem to come near the Scripture, and are like it as alchemy is like gold. A pregnant instance of this we have in 2 Thessalonians 2:1–2 and 2 Peter 2:1. Some false teachers (for Satan has his apostles and ministers as well as Christ) came with the plausible doctrine of mortification; for what could tend more to mortification than thoughts of the nearness of the Day of Judgment. And to strengthen this opinion, they pretend that they came to the knowledge of this truth partly by revelation from the Spirit, partly by computing the years, and partly by something the apostles had written.

Now, what was there in this opinion that was hurtful? It is an opinion that comes very near Scripture. Does not Peter say almost the same thing? "Be sober and watch, the end of all things is at hand." Nay, does not Paul say the very same thing? 1 Corinthians 10:11: "The ends of the world are come." That notion tends much to mortification and the practice of holiness. Do you think men would not live holily if they apprehended the Day of Judgment to be near? Would not this keep down an abundance of corruption? How Jerome professed himself to be overawed with this, that he thought he heard the sound of the last trumpet whatsoever he was a doing?

But to expose this wile, let me again tell you wherein it differs from Scripture, and then let me show the danger of it.

First, it differs from Scripture in that the word Peter uses is "approaches," and Paul says "the ends of the world are *coming*." But the word Paul uses that allows them to express their opinion by can mean that it shall be upon them who are living, as Grotius says, "this year." The word in other places is used for things present, such as 1 Corinthians 3:22, "all *are* yours," or "things present," in Romans 8:38. So these false teachers said that the day of the Lord is upon us. Their drift was to bring the day of the Lord within such a small space, as within a year or few months.

Second, the danger of it lay in what Satan might get by it. To show the harm this opinion might do, consider that Satan might aim at three things by it:

• It might occasion liberty in sin. Some might reason as they did in 1 Corinthians 15:32: "Let us eat and drink, for tomorrow we shall die." The rage of wicked and ungodly men might put them into excess of riot.

Revelation 12:12: "Satan himself hath great rage, knowing his time is but short." And so wicked men, when they know their time is short, and know that they have but a little space to take their fill of sin in, might be brought to a greater animosity against what was good, and to a greater excess in all that was evil.

• It might work a great deal of consternation and dejection in weak Christians, whom the very thoughts of so great and sad a day approaching might either with trembling, fear, or many jealousies overwhelm.

• The main end was to weaken the authority of Scripture. Allow for but one lie in Scripture and all its authority will fall to the ground. Let it be once entertained or taught by Scripture or divine revelation that Christ shall come at such a time, and that time proves to be false, then faith comes to be weakened. The delay of Christ's coming bred scoffing in some (2 Peter 3:4), and made others say that there is either no resurrection, or that it is past already.

Thus Augustine, in his *80 Epistles*, writing to Hesichius, who was troubled in this way, and was apt to think that the day of judgment might be at hand, advised him to beware how he leaned to such opinions, reproaches, and insults of enemies. Augustine warned him that many weak ones would be drawn by them from the Christian faith; and they would say there was no more certainty in the thing itself than in the prediction that it should be so suddenly. Then he added, "The doctrine of Christ's speedy coming is more desirable, but the mistake is more dangerous." So that the danger is that a man may call into question many other truths, as well as them which before he thought he believed.

Therefore let me speak to you who are Christians: do not think those doctrines that *seem* to come near and be like the Scripture may presently be entertained or hearkened to; but be sure that they come up to the

Scripture, and are adequate to the rule. If not, they are in no wise to be hearkened unto.

Oh, that we had in this the zeal and affection of our forefathers, who contended for the truth so much that they would not lose an iota or tittle of it. The Council of Nicea would not gratify Arius to alter even a letter in words regarding Christ's divinity. He would grant Christ was of a like substance as God, but not the same substance. By the sound he seemed to come near the truth. But as two men upon the top of two mountains seem so near they can shake hands, but must go a great way before they meet, so it is here. They seem near the truth in words, but were a great way off it. The Nestorians, in acknowledging the Virgin Mary, changed only a letter in the Greek word to describe her, but it made a wide difference in that she was called "Christ-bearing" rather than "God-bearing." The Latin and Greek churches, in the procession of the Holy Ghost, differed only in a preposition. The Greek church would grant the Holy Ghost to proceed by the Son in the sense of through the Son, but not out of the Son; and so the Greek church added to the Nicene Creed. Truth must not be lost by things that come near it; if any doctrine does not come up to the Scriptures, it must be rejected. If it goes beyond them, it is straw and stubble on the foundation. If it falls short, it is error also. Remember that corrupt opinions, like change-lings, are many times laid in the place of the right child, which is truth. "O foolish Galatians," said the apostle, "who hath bewitched you that you should not obey the truth?" The metaphor was taken from those who use witchcraft and present false shapes to the eyes, as the witch of Endor did the likeness of Samuel to Saul. But remember this is a wile of Satan, who himself did not abide in the truth (John 8:44). Labor to have the signature of all divine truths imprinted on your minds. Truth is the food of the soul. It is the spouse of the understanding, by which it has issue. It is a part of that armor the apostle calls "armor of light." Converse then much with God, the Father of Lights (James 1:17); with the Word, which is a book of light; with the saints, the children of light, if you would escape this wile.

DEVICE 10. When these things will not do, then, under pretense of lifting up the Spirit and revelations, Satan labors to cry down the Word of God and all the ordinary ministerial offices Christ has appointed in His Church, so that all doctrines and explications of Scripture are dismissed and rejected. Our first worthy reformers found a bitter conflict herein, for they no sooner had prevailed to restore the gospel, and expel the darkness of popery in Germany, and other parts, but straitway Satan sowed his tares. They called those who adhered to the Scriptures "literalists," and thereby made the work of reformation odious, as Eli's sons made the sacrifices of the Lord to be abhorred. As in superstitious times he kept down the truth by superstition and pompous ceremonies, so in times of reformation by pretended revelations and teachings elevated above the Word. The apostle aims at this when he says in 2 Corinthians 11:14 that Satan transforms himself into an angel of light. This delusion I speak of because in these times wherein reformation has been much pretended, the world, by pretenses of revelations and impulses of the Spirit, has cast off the Word. This art he applies in two ways:

First, some are mere pretenses, when wicked and wretched miscreants purposefully and knowingly use this way as a pretense to color all their wickedness. Thus Mohammed, to color his wickedness in the seducing the people, pretended the fits of the falling sickness he was troubled with to be certain ecstacies and ravishments at the appearance of the Angel

Gabriel, and the dove picking the corn out of his ear to be the appearance of the Holy Ghost. And thus oftentimes those who use such cursed pretenses come to be admired and esteemed who otherwise would have been accounted as nought.

Second, Satan applies this subtlety by deluding the fancies of men with a concurrence of pride and self-admiration so as to entertain thoughts that none know so much of God, nor have such secret communion with Him, as they, and that thereby they have sundry particulars above all the world revealed to them. Thus some have magnified themselves in particulars that have been revealed to them that have come to pass.

Acosta the Jesuit tells us of one who was a very great scholar, and who, through delusions and fancies, fell into such a conceit that he believed he had holiness given to him above angels, and that he was the savior of the world in regard of efficacy, and Christ only in regard of sufficiency; that he had the hypostatic union offered to him, and that he refused it. Thus Satan puffs men up with pride so that he may make them instruments of confusion and ruin to the church. Therefore, as an antidote against this, keep to the Word. 2 Peter 1:19: "You have a more sure word of prophecy." Notwithstanding all Satan's stratagies to adulterate it by heretics, to destroy it by tyrants, to debase it by profane scoffing at it, yet hold to the Word. "If they speak not according to the Word, it is because there is no light in them."

DEVICE 11. The eleventh wile by which Satan wins and allures many, to the hazard and peril of their eternal welfare, is by the working many lying signs, wonders, and miracles. These false signs look as if God, for the advantage of His gospel, did, at the first publishing of it, confirm it with many miracles and wonders (Hebrews 2:4). So Satan, to better facilitate a belief to his lies and falsehoods, puts forth much of his power in working lying signs and miracles. This the Scripture often expresses as a policy he uses above all. Matthew 24:24: "For there shall arise false christs, and false prophets, and shew many signs and wonders."

In Revelation 13:13 and 2 Thessalonians 2:9 the coming of that man of sin is described to be after the working of Satan, "with all power, and signs, and lying wonders." These words imply both the manner and the means of antichrist's working. First, the manner of antichrist's working is after the way and manner of Satan's working; that is, it holds proportion to that way that he usually takes. Second, it is by the means of Satan: as a fast friend of antichrist he puts out his power on his behalf for the working many lying signs and wonders.

They are called lying signs and wonders in two respects. First, in regard of their formality, they lack that which constitutes a true miracle. For a miracle, truly called, is doing some extraordinary work that runs into the senses exceeding the power of any creatures, as to make the sun stand still in the heavens by a word. All Satan's workings are but sometimes a deceiving of the sense, as Pharaoh's magicians; sometimes a deluding of the fancy; sometimes there is an exposing of secret things of nature to the sense of the ignorant, who do not know the depths of nature, and so think it a wonder; sometimes by applying of actives to passives, all which fall short of miracles. Second, they are called lying in regard of the end of them: they tend to draw from the truth, and therefore are not to be credited (Galatians 1:8).

DEVICE 12. The twelfth subtlety of Satan is to assault and afflict Christians with such temptations as, to their knowledge and experience, are unheard of, which perhaps they never heard any others to be tempted to, nor believe that ever any but themselves have had experience of. This Parisiensis calls temptations that they cannot parallel or sample. Now when Christians are exercised with such temptations, it exceedingly amazes them, as new engines and weapons not before seen by soldiers in former fights amaze the soldier and take away his courage. As new diseases, of which physicians have had no experience, most trouble them, and oftentimes discourage both patients and physicians, so oftentimes new temptations most amaze and sadden the soul.

Hence come those complaints tempted ones utter, "Nobody was ever as troubled as I am. Who was ever assaulted with such blasphemous thoughts, such atheistic injections, as I dare not speak or mention? Surely, if I were not worse than others, I would not have such thoughts; if I were not forsaken of God, He would not suffer me to be this tempted." But in this case you must remember what Paul said in 1 Corinthians 10:13: "There is no temptation happened to you but what is common to man." I may truly say to such, though they think it is new, yet it is that which some Christian or an other has experienced. You know what Elijah said to God, and what God's answer was. Elijah said, "I am left alone, and they seek my life." But God's answer to him was, "I have reserved to Myself seven thousand men." So you may think you are alone in this or that temptation, but, alas, there are a thousand in the militant church that are afflicted with the same temptations and stratagies of Satan.

DEVICE 13. The thirteenth wile is about holy duties. Satan puts us to do good duties upon wrong ends, which wholly alter their property. It is a true axiom in philosophy, "What the form is in natural things, the end is in moral ones." In moral things the end specificates the action. Jehu's slaying of Ahab's children was not obedience, but murder, though done by God's command (Hosea 1:4). God required it as a righteous satisfaction to justice, but Jehu did it out of ambition. Therefore God said, "I will avenge the blood of Jezreel upon the house of Jehu." Alms are good when they come like oil that makes no noise, but not when a trumpet is blown before them. Prayer is good when it comes from zeal, but it is but howling when it comes from lust (Hosea 7:14). Worshipping God is good, but if it is for base ends it is but self-seeking. Oh, therefore look to all duties. God must not only be the object, but the end. Worship must have no end below itself.

When Satan cannot hinder from duty, then he endeavors to spoil them. He will excite to duties, but to do them unseasonably. It is the commendation of a duty when it is done in season. Psalm 1 says that the blessed man brings forth his fruit "in due season." Now, when he cannot put out the candle, he will make it sparkle and flair (as in Martha, Luke 10:40–41), or he will turn affection the wrong way. The Jews were zealous for the Law, so Satan stirred that zeal against the gospel. Saul had a conscience of serving God (1 Samuel 13:12), and Satan forced him to offer sacrifice. The Corinthians were at first too remiss towards the incestuous Corinthian, and afterwards too severe. If Satan sees some heat, he drives it on too much. He will make us tyrannize in some service, and some duties he will make tyrants unto us. His aim is, by marrying religion and tyranny, to discourage men from religion.

His design is to press Christians with some violent assault when they are preparing themselves for duty, or to afflict them so in the duty that it may be rather their work to keep off the fowls from the sacrifice than to give up themselves to God in the duty as they should do. Therefore he presses Christians with extraordinary discouragements when they are to perform extraordinary

duty so that, if he cannot keep them from ordinary duties, he may keep them from extraordinary ones, and
labors to make them so uncomfortable that many are
afraid to perform them. Thus many are kept month after month, and year after year, from ever meddling with
the Lord's Supper (even those who will regularly pray
and hear) through the violent assaults of Satan, so that
some have given over duties for a kind of ease rather
than be so assaulted.

All I shall say to this is, whatever your discouragements are, do not give in to him. Satan may embitter a
sweet duty by his temptations, but he shall not make it
ineffectual; while you are wrestling and striving, his design is but by this violence to make you give up, to
choose rather to walk in a kind of peace than to maintain a war in the performance of duty.

DEVICE 14. The fourteenth wile Satan uses is to allow false remedies to prevail. The devil suggests these
to keep men from the true ones, and tells men, as
Samson did Delilah, if so and so is used, he shall be
overcome. Thus the Jews used their phylacteries, as
remedies against enchantments. And those two commandments upon which Christ said hang the Law and
the Prophets, the Christians did, from the superstitious
Jews, write them in schedules, and hang them about
their necks, as little gospels; but those were to be laid
up in the heart, not to be worn about the body. So the
Papists use salt, spit, and holy water in their exorcisms,
but these the devil, that hellish leviathan, esteems less
than the leviathan in Job 41:27 does of iron, which he
esteems as straw, and of brass as rotten wood. Beware
then of his counterfeit weapons. Do not think that
these things will frighten the devil; rather look up to
God, as David did, who prayed that God would turn the
counsel of Ahitophel to foolishness (2 Samuel 15:31).

DEVICE 15. The fifteenth wile of Satan is to make

false syllogisms, by which he works upon the guilt of conscience; and this consists in laying to our charge sins of omission or commission, in which the major or minor premise is false. He will lay to our charge many particular sins and corruptions committed by us—such as pride, hypocrisy, self-interest, and many duties omitted or overtly done—which temptation, if drawn in a syllogism, either the first or second proposition is false.

For example, "He in whom such a sin reigns as hypocrisy is is not the child of God. But such a one are you; therefore you are not a child of God." The minor premise here many times is false. It is true, a child of God cannot be a hypocrite, but he may have hypocrisy in him. The best way therefore to resist this temptation is to examine whether hypocrisy reigns in you. But Satan will press you on this by aggravating the evil and underrating the good so that he may bring men into trouble. Sometimes he makes false major premises, such as, "To relapse into the same sin is not compatible with grace." And for the examination he gives false rules and standards to judge by. Thus he troubles weak Christians about their graces and comforts by false syllogisms. He aggravates their imperfections in the former, tells them what falls they catch when they would run; what distractions they meet with when they most intend their minds, and asks how God's pure eye could behold these things with delight.

Now to discover the fallacy of this argument, you must know that we are not to place the strength of our confidence in our own righteousness, as if it would abide the severity of God's trial. For how can man be justified with God (Job 25:4)? So the perfection of our righteousness is not to be measured by the perfectness of the work, but by the uprightness of the will and the sincerity of the endeavor in aspiring towards perfection. Every failing does not make a man a hypocrite.

Jehoshaphat had many failings. He made a league of
amity with Ahab (2 Chronicles 18:3). He went to
Ramoth Gilead with him, notwithstanding Micaiah's
prophesy against it (2 Chronicles 18:27–28). Though
reproved by Jehu the Prophet, he joined in a special
league with Ahaziah, Ahab's son (2 Chronicles 20:35).
He bestowed his son upon Ahab's daughter (2 Chronicles 21:6). And yet God reckons him to be a holy man
(1 Kings 22:43). It is said, "He turned not aside from
that which was right in the sight of the Lord." If therefore obedience is interrupted, do not cast away your
confidence. "If any man sins, we have an Advocate with
the Father, Jesus Christ the Righteous." You have to do
with a God who will make your works at last more than
at first.

So in point of comfort Satan argues: "If you had
faith, you would have joy and peace; but you have no joy,
therefore you have no faith. 1 Peter 1:8 says, 'Believing,
ye rejoice.' " Now to answer this we are to know that
faith is the root upon which all true joy grows; it is the
flower whereof that is the stalk—but it is not always to
be found flourishing upon it.

There are three seasons when joy is most eminent,
and when God most abundantly dispenses it:

• In young Christians, in lambs whom He carries in
His bosom (Isaiah 40:11), with joy and comfort that they
may be strengthened. God would not carry Israel by the
way of the Philistines (Exodus 13:17) lest the people see
war and repent.

• After great storms, God makes broken bones to rejoice. Psalm 51:8: "Make me to hear joy and gladness,
that the bones Thou hast broken may rejoice." After
storms come the greatest calms; after His children have
been in the depths, He gives the greatest exaltations.

• When God calls men to witness His truth. In Acts
27:23, when Paul was to appear before Caesar, God sent

an angel to comfort him. We must consider that there may be the root when there is not the fruit; that which faith is to look at is what the gospel reveals. Now the gospel does not reveal that we shall have no sorrow or trouble, but that the covenant of peace shall not be removed from us (Isaiah 54:10).

DEVICE 16. The sixteenth device of Satan is to persuade Christians whom he thus afflicts to heed his counsel, so as either through shame or fear they dare say nothing. Some men who have foul diseases would rather die than tell the physician. They are like the Lacedemonian boy who allowed the fox to eat out his bowels, and would not reveal it. So many suffer temptations to eat out their hearts. Thus Satan wounds, and would not have Christians complain; he tempts and solicits, and would not have Christians to ask counsel; so many times the burden falls heavier, and the wound smarts all the more. Whereas if experienced Christians were acquainted with them, it might be a help to them; as wind stifled in the bowels of the earth shakes it, but finding passage does no harm, so oftentimes the very opening the devil's temptations is enough to scatter them. We should therefore seek remedy by communicating our grief to wise Christians who will pray for us and not deride us. Do not gratify sin in that which it loves so well, which is to be concealed and hidden.

DEVICE 17. Satan assaults us in such temptations wherein we least suspect ourselves, and to which perhaps neither constitution nor any custom of ours carries us, but only the present occasion draws forth our corruption. Thus men who are many times by nature patient and exceeding caring, are yet suddenly transported into becoming cruel. Thus Theodosius the Emperor, upon a mere passion, one of his soldiers suffering an injury, put to death at least three thousand in Thessalonica. Some of the ancients are of the opinion that the devil stirred up the Israelites to make the golden calf so that he might put Moses in a heat, who was the meekest man, that he might break the tables of the Law, and might not reprove their sin. Therefore suspect yourselves prone to every sin; do not repose anything upon constitution or temperament.

DEVICE 18. Satan assaults by giving hopes of returning out of sin by a speedy repentance and a timely revocation. But where is the promise of return? Are there not rather dreadful threatenings of permitting such to go on to final apostacy? It is easy to throw yourself headlong from the pinnacle of the temple, but you cannot keep yourself from falling without a miracle. Our hearts are like springlocks: they will shut by themselves, but will not open without a key. Augustine said, "It is no commendation to stand on the pinnacle, but to keep our standing and not to fall when we are in such danger is."

DEVICE 19. Satan will endeavor to keep any wounds that the Spirit has inflicted upon the conscience of any poor soul raw and smarting. It is true, Satan is not able to afflict immediately and really the conscience of a man, any more than he is able to comfort a man's conscience. As it is God's prerogative to know the heart, so it is to afflict and comfort the heart. But Satan may help to keep the wounds raw by disturbing the fancy, and filling them with horror and terror. He may shake and rattle the chains, though he cannot put them on upon any poor soul, and thereby keep them from the comfort which is their portion. Therefore, when terrors so frighten as to prejudice all medicines, we may suspect the hand of Satan in them.

DEVICE 20. Satan draws aside the soul to some sin when it is in the pursuit of some great mercy, or near the enjoyment of it, that so either their hands may be weakened in the pursuit and give over through the ap-

prehensions of their own guilt, which always weakens
confidence, or else may help to spoil the sweetness of it
in the enjoyment. Thus when Israel was nigh the enjoy-
ing of a great blessing, the land that God had
promised, upon the borders they fall to murmuring by
their hearkening to the spies who had brought an evil
report upon the land. Numbers 13:32–33: "It is a land
that eateth up the inhabitants, and the people that we
saw in it were men of a great stature, and there we saw
the giants." So that hereby they neglected the duty, and
set the mercy at a low rate. So that those who are beg-
gars, and expecting any great mercy, need to be watch-
ers too.

DEVICE 21. Satan will seek to make the duties of a
Christian's general and particular calling interfere and
clash one with another. There is a double calling in
which every man is set: There is a general and a particular calling, it is termed our general calling not only
for its extent, but because the things we are called to
are but one and the same, and common to all. We are
called to the same duties, to the same promises, to the
same profession of faith. The particular calling is that
in which men are not called to one and the same duty,
but act according to various gifts—one in this employment, another in that.

Now both these are to be performed regularly, and
the excellency of a Christian is when he so orders his
particular calling that it does not eat up the time that is
due to his general calling, and when he so orders his
general calling that it does not take away the time that
God has allotted for his particular calling.

Satan's great art is to disturb Christians in the performance of these. Some therefore are never quiet but
when they are hearing or praying; but their particular
callings and relations they almost never mind. This is
Satan's design, to disturb them by putting them upon

prayer when diligence is required in their particular calling. Others he takes off from hearing, and praying, and those duties which belong to Christians as such, under the pretense that they must provide for their families. He insinuates that while they care for their bodies, they may altogether neglect the care of the inward man. Therefore know that it is a great part of a Christian's prudence, and that which affords a great deal of comfort, to duly manage both callings. Do not let the time of your callings devour the time of your duties, but let your soul have its portion of your time as well as your body. Separate, then, your souls for a season to go up in the mount and converse with God, so that you may be more fit when you come down again to converse with men in your particular callings.

DEVICE 22. The last wile is that at which the text hints, an endeavor of Satan to bring us from one extreme to another so that we may be kept from the golden mean, wherein grace stands as well as virtue, which you know is seated between two vices, as Solomon's throne was between two rows of lions. And this device he uses in matters of sin, in matters of duty, and in matters of doctrine.

In matters of sin. Thus the incestuous Corinthian is first puffed up with pride and sins presumptuously, and then when, by the censures of the church, he is awakened to see his sin, he is well-nigh swallowed up with sorrow.

In religious duties. Satan either tempts us to a neglect of them, or to such a rigorous tyranny that makes many to groan under them and lie under woeful snares. And this device he accounts the more prevalent because we are apt to think oft times that the very work of grace lies in the highest opposition to that sin or vice that sits heaviest upon our hearts, when indeed sins and vices are not only opposite to virtues, but one to another. Be sure therefore that grace lies in a middle way. Sorrow for sin is not desperation; confidence in God is not presumption, but the middle way. Faith leaves both extremes and closes with God according to the rule of the Word.

In matters of doctrine. Basil, writing against Sabellius, to overthrow his heresy, uttered some inconvenient expressions about the Trinity. And Augustine, in his zeal against the Pelagians who slighted baptism, was carried out so that he pronounced those who died unbaptized not to be saved.

Chapter 5

Antidotes Against the Wiles of Satan

The next thing is to lay down some Scripture antidotes and preservatives against the wiles of Satan that
may keep you, not from being tempted by Satan, but
from being touched by the evil one, as Saint John
phrases it in 1 John 5:18: "that the evil one touch you
not." The word used there is the same word used in
1 Corinthians 7:1 regarding a man touching a woman.
The evil one does not touch him so as to produce his
own image and likeness upon him. Though I cannot
undertake such antidotes and preservatives as shall totally free you from his wiles, yet I can lay down antidotes
against his poison. These premonitions against his
subtleties, such Scripture armor against his rage and
malice, will, if used, keep you from being overcome by
him.

ANTIDOTE 1. Christian sobriety and watchfulness.
This we have from the Apostle Peter in 1 Peter 5:8: "Be
sober, be vigilant, because your adversary the devil
goeth about like a roaring lion, seeking whom he may
devour." Sobriety stands in a moderation towards the
things of this life. Pleasures, riches, and honors are the
usual baits with which Satan hides all his hooks and
temptations so that they may not be easily discerned;
and an immoderate thirsting, a keen and eager ap-
petite after these things, is the ready way to bring a believer into the midst of snares. They who will be rich,
says the apostle in 1 Timothy 6:9, whose desires and appetites are filled with the great things of the world, fall
into many snares. The snares sometimes strain their

consciences by deceit; sometimes they are to do evil actions, to make the stream of their actions great by the blood of others.

But as we must be sober in tempering our hearts and affections, so we must be watchful, which is a duty required of us as Christians, but indispensably necessary as we are Christian soldiers engaged always in a war, though not always in battle. A Christian has no peace but in his conscience and the grave. Nay, it is an irreconcilable controversy; it is a war without a truce. Therefore a Christian's life is called a warfare; they are trained up not in the pleasures of the court, but in the hardness of the camp. Christ, who is their Head, is therefore called in Scripture a man of war (Exodus 15:3), a leader and commander of the people (Isaiah 55:4), and a captain (Hebrews 2:10). Christians, who are His members, are called soldiers. 2 Timothy 2:3: "Thou, therefore, as a good soldier of Jesus Christ endure hardship." Their course of life is called a fight (2 Timothy 4:7). They who oppose them are enemies (Luke 1:71). Their temptations are assaults (1 Peter 2:11). This, as Chrysostom said, is confirmed by the authority of God Himself. Genesis 3:15: "I will put enmity between thy seed and the seed of the serpent." Therefore we must carry ourselves as soldiers and maintain our watch.

Now, though watching in the first meaning relates to the body, and implies more than to awaken from sleep—for it is a heedful care, and observing any thing we desire to keep safe—yet in a metaphorical sense it is applied to the mind, and so it is a circumspect and wise care in observing the frame and deportment of the whole soul. It is first a circumspect care, so those two words the apostle uses as our prayer import. Ephesians 6:18 signifies such a watching as not to lay the eyes together; it denotes not the least tendency to sleep. It is a military kind of term, said Grotius, taken from the watchings in war, which are usually most strict. In Colossians 4:2 it is such a watching wherein men stir and rouse themselves up.

It is also a wise care; watching is nothing but the exercise of prudence. And this watching must be of the whole soul; every faculty must be observed. As on every avenue there is a sentinel, so on every faculty there must be a watch.

And have we not a need to thus watch against sin and unto duty? Shall Satan be watchful and we be drowsy? Shall he continually go about seeking whom he may devour, and we not be circumspect to consider how we may deliver ourselves out of his paws? It was certainly an upbraiding to the disciples in Mark 14:37: "Simon, sleepest thou? Could you not watch with Me one hour?" Judas did not sleep. They were not so diligent to save their Master as Judas was to betray Him. And is it not a great reproach to a Christian that he is not as watchful to save himself as the devil is to destroy him?

Exercise watchfulness over your corrupt natures; the devil may tempt us, but he cannot hurt us without our consent. He may persuade, but he cannot compel. Our corrupt nature is the tinder upon which Satan strikes all his sparks. As birdlime is made from the dung of birds, so Satan's snares are made out of the dispositions that are in the heart to sin. The alchemists who boast of turning iron into silver and copper into brass assign the ground from the subalternation of metals, that there is a disposition in those metals to receive the highest quality of the other. So Satan forms his temptations upon our innate disposition; he draws out into act those latent dispositions in us.

Watch over the master sin, the bosom sin; watch strictly over this one.

ANTIDOTE 2. Resolution and Christian courage are as necessary as watchfulness. Watchfulness is good to prevent evil, and Christian resolution is necessary to undergo it. We need resolution, for he who will be a Christian must expect opposition; we must not think to pass out of Egypt without Pharaoh's pursuing us, or to travel through the wilderness of this world without opposition from these Amalekites. Satan will be in arms against us if he perceives even the thought of our departure. Once we have any holy resolutions, he will persecute us, as he did the woman in Revelation 12.

Therefore be resolute. The apostle exhorts us to this in Ephesians 6:10–11: "Finally, brethren, be strong in the Lord, and in the power of His might. Put on the whole armor of God." Why? "That you may be able to stand against the wiles of the devil." Take up resolution in the name of Christ to hold out. In Judges 20:22, the men of Israel encouraged themselves and set the battle again in array. Bernard says of Satan, "He more willingly pursues than fights, and he is more bold when we turn our backs than when we set our faces against him." Courage and constancy will bring victory. If you resist, you overcome; he may persuade, but he cannot force.

Eve complained in Genesis 3:13 that the serpent deceived her, not that he constrained her. Satan therefore chose the serpent for his form not because it was the strongest beast in the field, but because it was more subtle.

To encourage ourselves, consider that we have a better Captain and better armor. Satan fights with fleshy weapons, but the weapons of our warfare are not carnal, but mighty through God. Our own resolution is nothing without God. Satan knows there is nothing so mutable as man; it is as proper to him, as immutability is to God. And also, we have a better reward.

ANTIDOTE 3. The third antidote in resisting the wiles of Satan is to make use of the Lord Jesus Christ, first, as a pattern to know how to resist temptations, and, second, as an aide and succour.

First, in resisting temptations, make use of Christ as a pattern. He did combat with Satan to teach us to combat. The first promise God made to fallen man was that the seed of the woman would bruise the serpent's head (Genesis 3:15). And the first work Christ undertook after His solemn inauguration into His office was to fulfill this promise (as we see in Matthew 4) by entering the field, and coping with him and all the powers of darkness in a single duel. Now, as Abimelech said to his followers in Judges 9:48, "What you have seen me do, that do you," so Christ our Captain bids us look unto Him, and to observe him in these four particulars:

• Observe the weapon Christ chose to foil him by, and to resist all the temptations of Satan with. He could as easily, by His power, have rebuked and silenced him as he did the winds and waves, but He did it by the Word; to a variety of temptations He used just one weapon, the Word. Against temptations to distrust, against temptations to presumption, and to blasphemy, Christ said, "It is written, 'Man liveth not by bread.' And again it is written, 'Thou shalt not tempt.' "

Now in this let Christians take Christ as an example to resist Satan's suggestions by the Word. Take your arrows from that quiver, your advice from that unerring Oracle: "Thy word have I hid in my heart that I might not sin against Thee" (Psalm 119:11). The Word both discovers wiles and then fortifies against them. It first discovers all the temptations of Satan; it is a crystal glass in which you may see all the turnings and windings of this old serpent. Bernard compares Christians who are diligent in the Word to those doves in Song of Solomon 5:12 that sit by the waters because they can in them the better discern the motion of the hawk in the heavens. So the Word discovers the snares of Satan. When Joshua and the Israelites were not careful to ask counsel of God, they were caught by the policy and craft of the Gibeonites. And when you neglect to consult with God and His Word, no wonder the policy of Satan prevails against you! Jeremiah 8:9: "They have rejected the Word of the Lord, and what wisdom is in them?"

The Word also fortifies against the wiles of Satan, and furnishes believers with many weapons and arguments against them. If he promises great things, and so would seduce you that way, look into the Word, and there are better things than he can promise. For Satan can promise nothing but either you have it already (and the same water is sweeter from the fountain than when it passes through a sink) or you have better. You walk among fewer snares; you have an overabundance of spiritual goods for your defect of earthly ones. Consider, the offers of Satan are not for comforts but snares, not for the use of life but the provisions for sin. If he threatens, look into the Word; there are greater and sadder threatenings. What is his wildfire to fiery indignation, to snares, fire and brimstone, a horrible tempest that the Lord threatens to rain down upon sinners (Psalm 11:6). In every way you are furnished by the Word.

Here let me commend to you the excellency of this weapon our Savior made use of. It is called by the apostle in Revelation 1:16 "the sword of His mouth," and by the Apostle Paul, "the sword of the Spirit." And there is no sword like this, as David said of Goliath's. All must give place to this. Alexander's sword cut the Gordian knot. Ehud's sword that killed Eglon King of Moab, must give place to this one, that cuts asunder all the schemes and snares of Satan. The power of the Word is seen in that, though it has all disadvantages to hinder its operation, yet the Word of God's mouth does not return void. If applied to great persons, it makes them tremble. Where the word of a king is there is power (Ecclesiastes 8:4), and who may say unto him, "What are you doing?" Yet with it Elijah wounds Ahab (1 Kings 21:19). Paul does but brandish it and Felix trembles, yet Felix was in his royal robes and Paul in his chains. Micaiah, a prisoner, pronounced death to Ahab in 1 Kings 22:28. The most secret sins the Word finds out, and cuts off the first risings and stirrings of them. The world always stomached it, yet the Word gets ground and is effectual. Augustine said, "Come to a man in a lethargy and pinch him; come to a man in a frenzy and tie him down. Both are angry, but both are cured." But, alas, how this spiritual weapon is neglected, undervalued, and abused!

Some men do not know the Word, and therefore have no weapon in their houses. They do not care that the Scriptures speaks anything to them. They are like that Cardinal whom Rivet mentions in his *Orthodoxus Catholicus*; after he had heard Beza's oration in the Possiac Convention, he said, "I would either he had been dumb or we deaf." Alcibiades gave a schoolmaster a box to his ear because he did not have Homer's *Works* in his school. How much more may we be angry with those who do not have the Bible in their houses?

Others undervalue the Scriptures, such as Politian, who rejected them as being unfit for his polished style, and yet spent all his time upon trifles. Calderinus dissuaded his scholars from reading the Scriptures, yet commented on Virgil's filthy prose of *Priapus*.

Take heed of despising the Word. Take heed of bringing to it proud hearts. As some wear swords to show their gilded pummels and velvet scabbards, so many use the Word for ostentation rather than to war off wicked suggestions with it.

• As you should observe Christ in the choice of His weapon, so make use of the skillfulness and aptness of Christ in the applying the Word to the temptation, and in making use of the Word against the variety of Satan's temptations. You may observe how aptly and readily Christ made use of various Scriptures in resisting temptations in Matthew 4:4. "It is written, man shall not live by bread alone," and therefore we should depend upon the Providence of God in the midst of difficulties. "It is written, thou shalt not tempt the Lord thy God" (verse 7), and therefore we should not presume to expect blessings without the use of means when God promises them to us. "It is written, thou shalt worship the Lord thy God" (verse 10), and therefore we must not blaspheme Him or give His honor to another.

All these Scriptures our Savior brings out of one book; they are all taken out of Deuteronomy. Now if one book will afford such plenty, what then will the whole book of God do? We should therefore furnish ourselves with a variety of Scriptures against a variety of temptations. A Christian who is well-skilled in the Word is like one who has a plaster ready to lay on as soon as the wound is made, and thereby the danger is prevented. Therefore study the Scriptures so that you may have antidotes against this and that temptation, that you may have the wherewithal to answer Satan.

[Johann] Alsted (in his *Cases of Conscience*) tells of a Johannes Gatius, who was so perfect in the Scriptures that it was thought if all the Bible had been lost yet it might have been in a great measure recovered by his dexterity and readiness in it. It is a great commendation to be ready in the Scripture, but to be so ready as to improve it upon all occasions against temptations is the glory and excellency of a Christian. Get a skill in the Word so that you may have it in a readiness and be able to apply it. It is true, knowledge is the eye of the soul, which must direct how it must be applied. Ignorant men pervert it to their own destructions; they wound themselves, not their enemies. General discourses are like the beams of the sun dispersed in the air, which warm and cheer; but particular application is like the beams collected in the burning glass, which unites the beams and makes them burn.

Apply the Word to yourself. If you are tempted to covetousness, remember that life does not consist in the abundance of things. If you are tempted to to uncleanness, the Lord knows how to preserve the wicked (2 Peter 2:10), especially those who walk after the flesh in the lusts of uncleanness. Hebrews 13:4: "Whoremongers and adulterers God will judge." If you are tempted to inordinate fear, apply Luke 12:4; if to distractions in troublesome times, apply Psalm 55:22: "Cast thy burden upon the Lord." Have the Word in readiness, like Solomon's worthies in Song of Solomon 3:8 who had their sword on their thigh, ready to come out of the sheath immediately, and labor for skill to manage it.

• Look to Christ as a pattern in His constancy in resisting temptations, and in His perseverance against renewed assaults. Our Savior was long in the field, for forty days together tempted (Mark 1:13). Those things that are recorded in Matthew 4 were *after* the forty days. When He had fasted forty days, *then* the Tempter came, and persuaded Him to turn stones into bread. The evangelists record only those chief and last temptations. Now let us learn from our Captain to fight a good fight without discouragement and without changes; though temptations change, yet let not us change. Though they are multiplied, yet let us keep at our warfare and maintain our courage.

• Make use of Christ as a pattern in the manner of resisting by proportioning the resistance to the rise and growth of temptations. When temptations rise higher and are more gross, then we are to be more earnest, proportioning our resistance according to the vileness and sinfulness of them. That temptation of Christ to blasphemy, Christ rejected and resisted in another manner than He did the two former ones. There He only answered, "It is written," but here He said, "Get thee behind Me, Satan." He not only resisted it by the Word, but expressed a loathing and an indignation. And so should we when temptations assault us that strike immediately at God's glory: we should express a loathing and abhorrence of them. Certainly, such temptations to atheism, murder, blasphemy, and such like, are best resisted by an abhorrence and loathing of them, not by disputing with them, as Parisiensis said.

Some temptations are resisted by flight, such as "flee fornication." Some are resisted by indignation, as a man has his anger moved when he is offered nothing near the worth of his commodity. So when a man is tempted for trifles to sin against God and hazard his soul, it is enough to resist such temptations with that interjection, "Fie, fie upon such filthiness; fie upon such blasphemy," and this is by many thought the safest way.

You must make use of Christ as your aide and succour as well as your pattern; not only as a pattern to know how to fight, but make use of His power and strength to fight the better. "Be strong in the Lord, and in the power of His might" (Ephesians 6:10). Hebrews 2:18 says that "He is said to be able to succor them that are tempted." Do not go into the battle alone, therefore. In profane duels, wherein men challenge one another in the field for small punctillios of honor, or perhaps for worse things (in which, as Bernard said, "One man mortally sins, and the other eternally dies"), they seldom appear without seconds so that they may

see there is no wrong done, and that they may call for
aid if need be. Much more should Christians, in this
divine conflict and wrestling with Satan, take Christ
along with them. We should not go in the strength of
our own resolutions or our own vows, but we should go
against Satan as David did against the Philistines in
1 Samuel 17, "in the name of the Lord." When we do so,
we always prevail, and when we do otherwise, we are always foiled. There is no conflicting with Satan but in
God's strength. Remember that Christ is able to succor.
He has an ability of sufficiency, and an ability that
arises from experience.

ANTIDOTE 4. The fourth antidote is to be abundant
in the use of prayer. As faith is the best of graces in resisting Satan, so prayer is the best of duties. The neglect
of prayer was the beginning of Saul's fall, as most of the
fathers interpret 1 Samuel 14:19, when Saul com-
manded the priest to withdraw his hand from the ark.
They say of the palm tree that all its strength lies on the
top. The same is true of a Christian: all his strength lies
above.

There is a threefold use of prayer:

As a duty, for prayer is an offering. The psalmist
compares it to incense in Psalm 141. A sacrifice is but a
visible prayer, and prayer is nothing else but an audible
sacrifice.

As a dignity, when a man abstracts himself from
earth and grows into a familiarity with God. It is a
Mount Tabor, wherein the soul has admirable transfig-
urations, and does not see Moses and Elijah, but God.

As a necessity, for God has left prayer as our city of
refuge, to which we can on all occasions flee. Paul
would have the Thessalonians to pray without ceasing
(1 Thessalonians 5:17), and the Ephesians to pray
always (Ephesians 6:18).

There is no duty at all times so seasonable and useful as prayer. When we want blessings, prayer is the key whereby we unlock the treasury of heaven and gain the blessings we need. When we are assaulted by Satan, it is one of the best weapons we can use to defend ourselves with. When David did not know how to withstand the wisdom of Achitophel, who was then as an oracle of God, he prayed, "Lord, turn the counsel of Ahitophel unto foolishness" (2 Samuel 15:31). So you should pray, "O Lord, turn the counsel of this hellish adversary into folly."

When Jehoshaphat was in a great strait, the captains of the enemy having beset him about (2 Chronicles 18:31), he cried out, and the Lord helped him, and moved them to depart from him. This now is our way, to take ourselves to prayer. Bernard excellently said, "Satan's temptations are grievous to us, but our prayers are far more grievous to him." You do not know how you wound his head with prayer when he bruises your heel with temptations.

Therefore be much in prayer; it works deliverance from men, from devils, from all the straits you can be surrounded with. For this cause, said the apostle in 2 Corinthians 12:8, "I besought the Lord thrice," that is, when he was under the buffetings of Satan. "Pray," Christ said, "that you enter not into temptation." So pray that you fall not under temptation when you are entered into it. Prayer delivers us out of temptation. Matthew 26:41: "Watch and pray that you enter not into temptation." Chrysologus said, "He is sure to go into temptation who goes not to prayer." In temptation it gives a supply of strength (Exodus 17:11). Moses's sword was stronger than Joshua's. And prayer binds all our armor together, for prayer is the armor of the armor; and though it has no distinct part to which it is applied, yet it must be used with every piece of armor, without which all the armor will be no armor at all.

ANTIDOTE 5. The fifth antidote is to take heed of giving place to the devil. It is the apostle's counsel in Ephesians 4:27. That is, do not yield the least compliance with any temptation of Satan's. Jerome said, "The thought of evil is letting the head of the old serpent in, by which he will quickly wind in his whole body."

When you parley with temptations, and take them little by little into your thoughts (which at the first rising you should spit at), the victory is half gotten by Satan. It is not good to let poison rest under the tongue; it should be immediately spit out. Dalliances with temptations have proved fatal unto many, of which many instances might be given. It is a remarkable saying of Solomon in Ecclesiastes 10:13, regarding a foolish man, "The beginning of the words of his mouth is foolishness, but the end of his talk is mischievous madness." If you admit one, the other will follow.

ANTIDOTE 6. Take heed of venturing upon the occasions of sin, and coming near the borders of temptation. Do not expose yourselves to them. Bernard said that he was preserved from sin in three ways: by withdrawing from the occasion, by having power given to resist, and by having his affections healed and changed. "For I would have," he said, "easily fallen into many sins, but God, having mercy on me, did not suffer such an occasion to apprehend me." Job said of himself (Job 31:1), "I have made a covenant with mine eyes; why then should I think upon a maid?" And Solomon bids those who are given to wine not to look upon it when it is red, when it gives its color in the cup, when it moves itself aright (Proverbs 23:31). Objects have in them a kind of efficiency, and they work the heart accordingly to good or bad as men are in themselves good or bad. Beholding Jesus Christ, and eyeing Him in His death and suffering is an excellent and powerful means to mortify lusts and corruptions. So to quicken any lust or corruption is to present the object to the sense and the mind, which suddenly awakens those corrupt dispositions and inclinations that are there, and calls them, out as the presence of the iron does that virtue that is in a magnet.

Some physicians say that every body has in it a natural balsam which will of itself heal any wound or hurt the creature has received, provided it is kept clean from external putrefaction. But we are so far from this natural balsam that we have in us a natural poison, that is, original sin, that receives corroborations, as it were, from every object and occasion. Thus the Scripture tells us that Eve, when in a state of innocence, saw that that fruit was good, and was thereby induced to taste of it; and the bitterness of it she found unanswerable to that what it promised to the sight.

Take heed therefore of coming near the borders of temptations; beware of objects and occasions that may enflame you. Our hearts are powder, and therefore we must take heed of sparks. Do not give an indulgence, nor liberty to the eyes. When Solomon played the critic, he did not withhold his eyes from whatsoever he desired (Ecclesiastes 2:10). But when you are to do the office of Christians, you must circumscribe and confine your eyes and other senses. And if you would mortify your eyes, then mortify your hearts; the eye and the heart have a great sympathy to each other. The way to keep yourselves from being hurt by objects and occasions is to keep the heart pure, to subdue sin there. Laying the medicine to the heart is like putting it to the wound. The other is like laying it to the weapon, which is not so natural. We must therefore lay a strict law upon every member of our body, yet we must not think so to look to the heart as to neglect the outward man. In navigation, cosmography is no less useful than astrology, because all the observations of the stars are in reference to the earth, and to the place to which they sail. And in our spiritual voyage to heaven, it is no less requisite that we study the map of our own earth than to study the globe of heaven where we are sailing.

ANTIDOTE 7. The seventh antidote against the wiles of Satan is diligence and industry in your calling. While the bird is flying it is safe, but when it sits and perches upon a tree it becomes an object for any instruments wherewith to shoot and destroy it. And so it is for a Christian: when he is busy in his calling he is in a great measure safe from temptations, but when he becomes idle, and does not busy himself in that station God has set him in, he becomes fit ground and soil for Satan to sow any temptation and lust in. Idleness exposes the soul to all its spiritual enemies; and whereas it is the devil's business to tempt us, it is an idle man's business to tempt the devil. It is a good answer to the devil when he tempts to sin, "It is not lawful to do it." But it is a stronger answer, and a better one in some's opinion, "I am not at leisure. I cannot attend such motions." Such answers put Satan beyond his usual arts; they put him more to a loss. He would much rather enter a dispute about the lawfulness of something than be turned off with, "I am not at leisure."

It is a golden rule divines give to tempted persons, to be diligent in their callings. It was Jerome's advice to his friend Rusticus to be always doing some good so that the devil might always find him employed. Think of this, you who run out of your callings, who neglect your callings, who think it a piece of bondage to be subject to a calling: alas, you are the nearer to temptation, and the more subject to be taken in his wiles. The misery of idleness is that an idle man is sometimes secure, but never safe. He is safe who is above danger, but he is secure who fears no danger.

ANTIDOTE 8. The eighth Scripture antidote is sincerity of heart, which many understand by the girdle of truth spoken of in Ephesians 6:14. "Truth in its latitude" is by some understood in this place, but I shall propose it in a double consideration: first, doctrinal, and so truth implies a conformity in our understandings to the will and mind of God. Truth in general is nothing but the conformity of one thing to another, whereof one is the sampler and the other the exemplification. The sampler or pattern is God, and the mind of God is His Word. And unto that ought everyone to have their judgment and understanding so conformed as to agree with it and not admit other impressions that are different from the Word of God. Thus in Scripture we are warned not to be tossed to and fro with every wind of doctrine (Ephesians 4:14), and to hold fast the pattern of wholesome words (2 Timothy 1:13).

Truth may also be morally considered, as it is opposed to hypocrisy, and so it is the correspondence of our outward actions to our inward affections; for as our inward affections must have their stamp from God, so must they endeavor to print their true stamp upon our actions. The seed that is sown in the ground bears the like seed above ground, and the fruit is not unlike the tree. No more should we, in our morality, sustain one person in our bosom and another in our countenance. This Aquinas calls simplicity. Cressolius refers simplicity to the topic of truth, from which it is only rationally distinguished, and informs us that it is called simplicity because it does not tend to divers things, as inwardly to intend one thing when outwardly it pretends another. This the Scripture holds forth in Joshua 24:14: "Fear the Lord, and serve Him in sincerity, and in truth." Psalm 51:6: "Thou lovest truth in the inward man."

Now as both these branches are included in this girdle of truth, so they are both necessary to withstand

the wiles of the Tempter. Get your judgments settled in
the knowledge of the truth so as not to be removed
from it as the Galatians were (Galatians 1:6), for it is the
method of Satan to hold forth false doctrines in the
similitude of divine truths, by which he deceives the
eyes of their judgments who are unstable in the ways of
God. He begins in the judgment that is first corrupted,
and then derives its contagion to other faculties; as the
bloodshot eye is first vitiated, and then represents all
objects of its own color. Be sure therefore to keep your
judgment sound. Oh, into what an abyss of error will
corrupt principles in the understanding lead men into!
But then labor also for sincerity and uprightness of
heart, which alone works constancy and perseverance.
Let there be no hypocrisy in your profession of religion. Labor to be Nathanaels and Jacobs. Get this in
opposition to double mindedness; diversity of interests
will make the mind unstable in all its actions. A dou-
ble-minded man, said the Apostle James, is unstable in
all his ways, like a wave of the sea, tossed to and fro. But
when the heart is sincere, and single in the ways of
God, when a man with a single eye looks at God and
His glory, he is greatly secured against Satan. Satan
cannot do with him as he does with another man. This
girdle of truth is his ornament and his strength.

ANTIDOTE 9. I will here lay down one general rule
or antidote drawn from war. Those who write about
rules and matters of war give this as general counsel:
Whatever is profitable to the enemy is hurtful to you,
and whatever is profitable to you is hurtful to your enemy. For his gain is our loss, his rise our fall, his honor
our shame, and his help our hindrance. Therefore
study with yourselves what that may advantage Satan in
any way, and be sure that it is hurtful for you. And if
there is anything profitable to you that is hurtful to
Satan—such as prayer, heavenly meditation, converse

with promises, society with the saints, all these, and many others like them—it must be good for us because it is detrimental to Satan.

ANTIDOTE 10. As a powerful antidote against Satan's temptations, have an eye often to Scripture encouragements. The war into which a Christian has entered, who wrestles with the prince and powers of darkness, is a fierce war; but you are not without encouragements in this war. If your enemy is great, God has furnished you with good armor. Put on then the whole armor of God (Ephesians 6:13). It is called God's armor because it is made by God. The Hebrew usually puts the name of God on things to note the excellence of them. No weapons will serve to fight against the devil but God's; nothing will make you shotfree but the armor of God.

Now, as your encouragement is in having this armor, so your safety lies in putting on all of it. It all has the same Maker. It is all the same metal, not like Nebuchadnezzar's image, where the head was gold and the breast was silver. All is equally precious, and all equally useful. Therefore put on your armor. If your enemy is subtle, you have an expert Captain. If the brunt and conflict is hard, look often to the crown that is promised (James 1:12). Will not a crown make a full recompense? Bernard said, "If here we are victorious, there we shall be glorious, having instead of a helmet a diadem, for a sword a palm, for a shield a cloak or mantle wrought with gold, for the breastplate the robe of delight. And is it not in the mean time better to be kept low than utterly ruined? Is it not better to bear the weight of our armor than feel the fiery darts of the malignant one? If you dread because Satan is a fiery serpent, remember that Jesus Christ is that Brazen Serpent who can heal all his stings. If you are afraid of his roaring because he is a devouring and roaring lion, remember that Jesus Christ is the Lion of the Tribe of Judah. He is a lion for valor as the other one is a lion for cruelty. You have then three great encouragements: your Captain is stronger, your armor is better, and your reward is excellent and glorious. And therefore when you think the pressure is hard, and the fight bloody, remember these things which used to encourage other soldiers, and should much more encourage Christian soldiers.

Now, do not lay up these antidotes on a piece of paper, as you usually do with antidotes that are prescribed by a physician, that you will use when you please; but use these continually. Have them near you in readiness. Satan is always tempting; he always has fiery darts about him, though he does not throw them. He is always biting at the heel; therefore be always ready to make resistance.

And do not think that these things are useful in times of great trial, but not now. This is a wile of Satan to keep you from profiting, and therefore look on what has been said as a call from heaven to awaken you to diligence in your Christian warfare, and to resist him who has many devices to destroy you, and who abounds in all subtlety and industry to bring his devices to pass.

Finis